LITTLE LATIN
READERS

LITTLE LATIN READERS
TEACHER'S GUIDE

Liber Primus

PUELLA ROMANA
(The Roman Girl)

Julie A. Collorafi

www.littlelatinreaders.com

www.littlelatinreaders.com

TABLE OF CONTENTS

COURSE DESCRIPTION (*Puella Rōmāna*)

COURSE OBJECTIVES (First Semester)

Master first declension feminine nouns in the nominative case

Introduce first declension masculine nouns in the nominative case

Master understanding of subjects and predicate complements

Master use of first declension nouns with prepositions governed by the ablative case

Master use of first declension nouns with prepositions governed by the accusative case

Master first declension feminine nominative and ablative singular and plural forms

Master the use of first declension feminine adjectives in nominative and ablative cases

Master the use of third person present indicative active of the being verb *esse*

Master the use of third person present indicative active intransitive first conjugation verbs

Master the use of the prepositions *in, ad, prope, super*

Master the use of first declension feminine adjectives in the nominative and ablative

Master noun/adjective agreement in first declension feminine nominative and ablative

SCOPE AND SEQUENCE

Quarter 1: Lessons 1-4

Quarter 2: Lessons 5-8

Quarter 3: Lessons 9-12

Quarter 4: Lessons 13-16

METHODOLOGY

The Little Latin Readers series follows the general outline of the first year of Fr. Henle's First Year Latin, extended over six years of elementary school, e.g., third grade through eighth grade. Puella Romana introduces the first declension. Britanni et Galli introduces the second declension and Civitates Europae introduces the third declension. Starting with Italia and ending with Sancta Missa, the fourth and fifth declensions are added along with more advanced grammatical concepts. The diagramming of sentences begins in the fifth level, Vita Mariae, and continues throughout. The use of verbs is confined in the first two levels to intransitive verbs and nominative, genitive and ablative endings are introduced. In this way, the range of endings is kept very small and more attention may be fixed upon the conceptualization of Subject-Verb agreement, along with Being Verbs, Intransitve Verbs and Predicate Complements. For the sake of variety a number of prepositional phrases and the genitive of possession are included.

The readers present short Latin reading selections for immersion. Drill books offer more detailed grammar explantions and vocabulary enrichment. For each lesson, a Latin quote from Scripture or the writings of the saints is presented for memorization. Diacritical markings are present in all books and drill books study the prōnunciation and accent rules so the student will become more adept at prōnunciation.

The Teacher's Guide gives detailed weekly lesson plans, based on a 4-day week with suggestions for boardwork during group lessons and suggested Latin prayers. Weekly quizzes test material in workbooks and drillbooks. Quarterly exams only test material from the workbook. The content of the drillbook is given not for mastery but for enrichment and to familiarize the student with concepts that will be studied in-depth on the next level.

Upon completion of all the levels, students will have been introduced and have extensive practice with all the material in Henle Latin I.

DESCRIPTION OF WEEKLY ASSIGNMENTS
AND THE WEEK'S DAILY COURSE PLAN

There are several elements in the **Weekly Course Plan**. The **Weekly Breakdown** summarizes the main concepts, along with the **Goals and Notes** to be covered in that week. The **Daily Assignments** for the student are given in the boxes indicated by **DAY 1, DAY 2, DAY 3** and **DAY 4.** Teacher/parent guidelines are given to the right side of the **Student Daily Assignments**. The plans are given for a 4-day week.

The **Puella Rōmāna** level contains lessons for 36 weeks, divided into four 9-week quarters. Bimonthly quizzes reinforce the material covered every two weeks. Extensive quarterly reviews are given for the student/parent's use before the mid-quarter and quarterly exams. Teacher/Parents should review each exam in advance and throughout the quarter.

It is recommended every class is begun with a prayer which is a fine opportunity for the students to memorize the prayers in Latin and to teach the meaning of the words. Repeat them for several weeks until they are known. Memorize the vocabulary words, definitions, and charts and review constantly for successful retention and comprehension.

With every weekly lesson this general format may be followed:

1) Read aloud the explanations in the workbook on the first page of each weekly lesson. Do not work on the exercise sets at this time.

2) Prōceed to the reader and go through the **New Words to Learn** page with the students. The teacher should prōnounce each word first and have the class repeat it together. At this point, the students might also copy each new word into a special notebook.

3) Prōceed to the story on the next page, allowing the students to take turns reading aloud the sentences or paragraphs in each selection. (Use of the online audio is also helpful at this time.)

Important: Do not offer translations until the entire story or selection has been read aloud so the children will hear the entire selection in Latin without any breaks into English. This will help aid the development of aural comprehension.

4) After the selection is read, go back over the story and take turns having the students re-read each sentence and translate into English, correcting as necessary.

5) After the reading is finished, if desired, the prōblem sets in the workbook can be reviewed orally in class as time permits and the rest assigned as homework.

6) The teacher may use the **Boardwork Suggestions** located in the back of the Teacher's Guide for classroom explantaions and exercises with students taking turns working on a whiteboard or chalkboard.

7) Review all vocabulary words and grammar definitions.

(I have found it very helpful to set up for each student a composition notebook or binder divided into sections with the Page Tabs on the last page of the workbook so the students may record in apprōpriate sections each new word as it is encountered. Important grammar definitions may also be copied as they come up in the workbook. Alternatively, flash cards could be made for each new word.)

HOMEWORK ASSIGNMENT: Complete all unfinished prōblem sets and review the reading selection with the online audio. Review entries in the notebook/ flashcards. Remind student to listen to the **New Words to Learn** and weekly story on the online audio.

DRILLBOOK: Classtime every week should be spent on the enrichment exercises in the drill book, as desired.

BOARDWORK SUGGESTIONS: Located at the back of the Teacher's Guide, these exercises are a valuable tool for explaining and reinforcing the weekly lessons. Excellent for engaging students and allowing the teacher to evaluate student's comprehension of the material.

LATIN PRAYERS FOR USE WITH PUELLA ROMANA
Learning the **Signum Crucis** (Sign of the Cross), the **Ave Maria** (Hail Mary), and the **Gloria Patrī** (Glory Be) is recommended for the first two levels. These three prayers are included in the drillbook for the students to study phrase by phrase. The teacher should write each on the board and have the children copy them into their notebook under the Page Tab, "Latin Prayers".

Recordings of all reading selections in the reader are available in the online audio. The online audio also aids the student in memorizing the grammar rules and definitions and in learning the correct prōnunciation of the Latin prayers and sayings. Watch for the picture of the headphones in the drillbook which indicates if the exercise has been recorded.

COURSE PLAN (FIRST QUARTER)
WEEK ONE

Weekly Breakdown	Goals and Notes for the Week
Prōnunciation, first declension feminine singular nouns	You should have basic understanding of ecclesiastical prōnunciation and the use of the **macron** which lengthens the accented vowel. Grammar concepts of nouns and declensions are presented.

	Student Daily Assignments	[X]	Parent Daily Guidelines
DAY 1	**LESSON ONE** Read p. 1, 3, 4 in workbook. □		(**NEEDED:** Workbook, drillbook, Teacher Guide.) **READ** p. 1 in the workbook aloud with students, explaining the concepts of nouns and declensions. **INTRODUCE puella** and **fēmina. READ** Exercises E, F, G, H with students on p. 3-4 of workbook. **READ** first declension nouns in Exercise I on p. 4 aloud with students.
	*HOMEWORK Complete exercises on p. 2 of workbook. □		HOMEWORK: Complete exercises on p. 2 of workbook.
DAY 2	Read p. 2-3 in reader. Read p. 4 in drillbook. □		(**NEEDED:** Drillbook, reader.) **INTRODUCE** *"New Words To Learn"* on p. 2 of reader with students. **HAVE STUDENTS READ** the two sentences on p. 3 of reader once through without stopping. **READ** each sentence again and ask for translations. Correct as necessary. **DISCUSS** new prayers and Latin saying on p. 4 of the drillbook.
	*HOMEWORK Reread story with online **audio**. Complete exercises on p. 4 of drillbook. Learn the **Signum Crucis** and Week 1 Latin Saying on p. 4 of drillbook. □		*HOMEWORK: Reread story with **online audio**. Write **Signum Crucis** and new Latin saying on p. 4 of drillbook.
DAY 3	Read p. 2-3 in reader. Read p. 2 in drillbook. □		(**NEEDED:** Drillbook, reader.) **DISCUSS** in class *"Definitions"*, *New Vocabulary Words"* and *"Synonyms"* on p. 1 of drillbook, introducing new noun **ancilla**. On p. 2, read "Accent Practice" with students and discuss *"Latin-English Cognates"*.
	HOMEWORK Complete p. 1 of drillbook. □		HOMEWORK: Complete exercises on p. 1 of drillbook.
DAY 4	HOMEWORK: Reread p. 2-3 of reader. Review vocabulary. Study Latin phrase and saying on p. 4 of drillbook. □ □		**DO** the exercises in the **Lesson One Boardwork Suggestions** on p. 78 of the **Teacher Guide** on the board with class. *HOMEWORK: Reread p. 2-3 of reader. Review vocabulary. Study Latin phrase and saying on p. 4 of drillbook.

WEEK ONE Grade Book				
ASSIGNMENTS	Include [X]	(A) Points Earned	(B) Possible Points	A/B x 100 = % (C)
Daily Asssignments	□		8	
WEEK 1 AVERAGE		Add up column C and divide by number of included [X] assignments =		%

COURSE PLAN (FIRST QUARTER)
WEEK TWO

Weekly Breakdown	Goals and Notes for the Week
Prōnunciation, first declension feminine singular nouns	You should have basic understanding of ecclesiastical prōnunciation and the use of the **macron** which lengthens the accented vowel. Grammar concepts of nouns and declensions are presented.

	Student Daily Assignments	[X]	Parent Daily Guidelines
DAY 1	**LESSON ONE** Read p. 2-3 in drillbook. *HOMEWORK: Complete exercises on p. 2-3 of drillbook. **STUDY** the **Signum Crucis** and "O Roma Felix" on p. 4 of drillbook.	☐ ☐ ☐	(**NEEDED:** Drillbook.) **DISCUSS** "The First Declension" on p. 2 of drillbook in class. **HAVE** students write the names of the five cases on the board. **READ** the "First Declension Nouns" on p. 3 with the class and help them find their English equivalents. **READ** "Latin Days of the Week" with students. *HOMEWORK: Complete exercises on p. 2-3 of drillbook. Study the **Signum Crucis** and the new Latin saying on p. 4 of drillbook.
DAY 2	Read p. 1-2 in workbook. *HOMEWORK: Reread story on p. 2-3 in reader with **online audio**. Complete exercises on p. 4 on workbook. Review the Signum Crucis and new Latin saying on p. 4 of drillbook.	☐ ☐	(**NEEDED:** Workbook, Teacher's Guide) **RE-READ** the prōnunciation **Exercises E, F, G, H** on p. 3-4 of workbook. **WRITE** the nouns on p. 4 from **Exercise I** on the board and circle the **-a** at the end of each noun. **REPEAT** exercises from the **Boardwork Suggestions** on p. 47 of Teacher's Guide as necessary. *HOMEWORK: Reread story on p. 2-3 in reader with **online audio**. Complete exercises on p. 4 on workbook. Review the Signum Crucis and new Latin saying on p. 4 of drillbook.
DAY 3	Read p. 1 and 4 in drillbook. Read p. 2 in workbook. *HOMEWORK: Reread story. Review definitions, vocabulary and new prayer and Latin saying.	☐ ☐	(**NEEDED:** Teacher's Guide, workbook, drillbook.) **REVIEW Grammar Questions** on p. 2 of workbook. **REVIEW** all definitions and vocabulary on p. 1 of drillbook. **puella, fēmina, ancilla, est.** **REVIEW** Latin prayer and saying on p. 4 of drillbook. *HOMEWORK: Reread story. Review definitions, vocabulary and new prayer and Latin saying.
DAY 4	Lesson One Quiz on p. 46 of the Teacher's Guide.	☐	**LESSON ONE QUIZ:** **VOCABULARY:** New vocabulary, p. 1 of drillbook. **GRAMMAR:** Grammar Questions, p. 2 of workbook. **LATIN SAYING AND PRAYER,** p. 4 of drillbook.

WEEK TWO Grade Book				
ASSIGNMENTS	Include [X]	(A) Points Earned	(B) Possible Points	A/B x 100 = % (C)
Lesson One Quiz	☐		6	
Daily Asssignments	☐		6	
WEEK 2 AVERAGE		**Add up column C and divide by number of included [X] assignments =**		%

Weekly Breakdown		Goals and Notes for the Week
Singular being verb **'est'**, subject, subject/verb agreement, conjugation of **'Esse'**		Be familiar with defintion of subjects, singular subject. singular being verb 'est' and subject/verb agreement. Learn the conjugation of 'esse' in present indicative active. Learn the adverb 'non'.
Student Daily Assignments	[X]	**Parent Daily Guidelines**
DAY 1	**LESSON TWO** Read p. 5-6 in workbook. *HOMEWORK: Complete exercises on p. 5-6 in workbook.	☐ ☐	(**NEEDED:** Workbook) **READ** p. 5 in workbook w/ students. **WRITE** sentences from **A. English Practice** on p. 5 on the board and let students circle the subject and tell if it is singular or plural. **DISCUSS** *"The Adverb Nōn"* on p. 5 and **B. Grammar Questions** on p. 6. HOMEWORK: Complete exercises on p. 5-6 in workbook.
DAY 2	Read p. 4-5 in reader. Read p. 8 in drillbook. *HOMEWORK: Reread story on p. 5 of reader with online audio. Complete exercises on p. 8 of drillbook.	☐ ☐	(**NEEDED:** Reader, drillbook) **READ** *"New Words To Learn"* on p. 4 of reader. **HAVE STUDENTS READ** story on p. 5 of reader once without stopping. Read each sentence again and ask for translations. Correct as necessary. **INTRODUCE** and discuss first phrase of *Ave Maria* and the new Latin saying on p. 8 of the drillbook. *HOMEWORK: Reread story in reader on p. 4-5 with **audio**. Complete p. 8 of drillbook.
DAY 3	Read p. 5 of drillbook. *HOMEWORK: Reread story. Complete all exercises on p. 5 of drillbook. Review **puella, fēmina, ancilla, nōn, est.**	☐ ☐	(**NEEDED:** Drillbook) **DISCUSS** the *"Definitions"* on p. 5 of of the drillbook. **EXPLAIN** *"Using Est in Sentences"* and *"Subject-Verb Agreement"* on p. 5 of drillbook with examples on the board. *HOMEWORK: Reread story with audio. Complete all exercises on p. 5 of drillbook. Review **puella, fēmina, ancilla, nōn, est.**
DAY 4	Read p. 8 of workbook. *HOMEWORK: Complete all exercises on p. 8 of workbook.	☐ ☐	(**NEEDED:** Teacher's Guide, workbook.) **COMPLETE** Lesson Two Boardwork Suggestions on p. 78 of the Teacher's Guide. **DISCUSS** the exercises on p. 8 of the workbook. **WRITE** sentences from **J. English-to-Latin** on board and help students compose Latin sentences. *HOMEWORK: Complete exercises on p. 8 of workbook.

WEEK THREE Grade Book				
ASSIGNMENTS	Include [X]	(A) Points Earned	(B) Possible Points	A/B x 100 = % (C)
Daily Assignments	☐		8	
WEEK 3 AVERAGE	**Add up column C and divide by number of included [X] assignments =**			%

Weekly Breakdown	Goals and Notes for the Week
Singular being verb **'est'**, subject, subject/verb agreement, conjugation of **'Esse'**	Be familiar with defintion of subjects, singular subject. singular being verb 'est' and subject/verb agreement. Learn the conjugation of 'esse' in present indicative active. Learn the adverb 'non'.

	Student Daily Assignments	[X]	Parent Daily Guidelines
DAY 1	**LESSON TWO** Read p. 6 in drillbook. *HOMEWORK: Complete exercises on p. 6-7 in drillbook.	☐ ☐	(NEEDED: Drillbook) **DISCUSS** *"The Latin Verb Esse"* on p. 6 of drillbook. **MAKE** chart of being verbs on board and have students fill it in. **HELP** students do the practice set on same page. HOMEWORK: Complete exercises on p. 6-7 of drillbook.
DAY 2	Read p. 4-5 in reader. Read p. 8 in drillbook. *HOMEWORK: Reread story on p. 5 of reader with online audio. Complete exercises on p. 8 of drillbook.	☐ ☐	(NEEDED: Reader, drillbook) **READ** *"New Words To Learn"* on p. 4 of reader. **HAVE STUDENTS READ** story on p. 5 of reader once without stopping. Read each sentence again and ask for translations. Correct as necessary. **INTRODUCE** and **DISCUSS** first phrase of **Ave Maria** and the new Latin saying on p. 8 of the drillbook. *HOMEWORK: Reread story in reader on p. 4-5 with **audio**. Complete p. 8 of drillbook.
DAY 3	Read p. 6-7 in drillbook. *HOMEWORK: Reread story. Complete all Lesson Two exercises. Study Latin saying on p. 8 of drillbook. Review **puella, fēmina, ancilla, nōn, est.**	☐ ☐	(NEEDED: Drillbook) **REVIEW** p. 6-7 in drillbook. **COPY** the Latin being verb chart on board. **REPEAT Boardwork Suggestions** as needed. Students may take turns writing the Latin prayers and sayings on the board. *HOMEWORK: Reread story with audio. Complete all exercises for Lesson Two in drillbook and workbook. Study Latin saying on p. 8 of drillbook. Review **puella, fēmina, ancilla, nōn, est.**
DAY 4	Take Lesson Two Quiz on p. 47 of the Teacher's Guide.	☐	**LESSON TWO QUIZ:** **VOCABULARY:** New vocabulary, p. 6 of workbook. **GRAMMAR:** Grammar Questions, p. 6 of workbook. **LATIN SAYING:** "Ego sum resurrectio et vita", p. 8 of drillbook. **CONJUGATION CHART:** Being verb "esse" on p. 6 of drillbook.

WEEK FOUR Grade Book				
ASSIGNMENTS	Include [X]	(A) Points Earned	(B) Possible Points	A/B x 100 = % (C)
Lesson Two Quiz	☐		15	
Assignments	☐		6	
WEEK 4 AVERAGE	**Add up column C and divide by number of included [X] assignments =**			%

Weekly Breakdown	Goals and Notes for the Week
Adjectives, proper nouns, common nouns.	Be familiar with defintion of adjectives, nouns, prōnouns. Know the difference between common and proper nouns. Begin learning about Latin personal prōnouns.

	Student Daily Assignments	[X]	Parent Daily Guidelines
DAY 1	**LESSON THREE** Read p. 9 of workbook. *HOMEWORK: Complete exercises on p. 9-10 of workbook. Learn new adjectives: **bona, Christiāna, opulenta, parva, pulchra, Rōmāna, longa**.	[ ] [ ]	(NEEDED: Workbook.) **INTRODUCE** *"First Declension Adjectives"* on p. 9 of workbook. **INTRODUCE** the six new adjectives: **bona, Christiāna, opulenta, parva, pulchra, Rōmāna, longa**. REVIEW *"proper nouns"* on p. 9 of workbook. Introduce 4 proper nouns (names) on p. 9 of workbook. *HOMEWORK: Complete exercises on p. 9-10 of workbook.
DAY 2	Read p. 6-7 in reader. Read p. 12 in drillbook. *HOMEWORK: Reread story on p. 7 of reader with online audio. Complete exercises on p. 12 of drillbook.	[ ] [ ]	(NEEDED: Drillbook, reader.) **READ** *"New Words To Learn"* on p. 6 of reader with students. **HAVE STUDENTS READ** story on p. 7 of reader once without stopping. **READ** each sentence again and ask for translations. Correct as necessary. **DISCUSS** new *"Ego Sum"* phrase, next phrase of **Ave Mari**a and new Latin saying. on p. 12 of drillbook. *HOMEWORK: Reread story on p. 7 of reader with online audio. Complete exercises on p. 12 of drillbook.
DAY 3	Read p. 9-10 in drillbook. *HOMEWORK: Complete p. 9-10 in drillbook. Study, prayers, phrase and new saying on p. 12 of drillbok.	[ ] [ ]	(NEEDED: Drillbook.) **REVIEW** *"Definitions"* and *"New Vocabulary"* on p. 9 of drillbook. **READ** *"Latin-English Cognates"* on p. 9. **DISCUSS** *"Using Latin Adjectives"* on p. 10. **HAVE** students write sentences on board and circle adjectives. *HOMEWORK: Complete p. 9-10 in drillbook. Study, prayers, phrase and new saying on p. 12 of drillbok.
DAY 4	Read p. 11 in workbook. *HOMEWORK: Complete p. ll in workbook. Study p. 9 and 12 in the drillbook.	[ ] [ ]	(NEEDED: Teacher's Guide, workbook, drillbook.) **DO** the **Lesson Three Boardwork Suggestions** in the Teacher's Guide on p. 78. **REVIEW** the new adjectives and 4 proper nouns. *HOMEWORK: Complete p. 11 in workbook. Study p. 9 and 12 in the drillbook.

WEEK FIVE Grade Book				
ASSIGNMENTS	Include [X]	(A) Points Earned	(B) Possible Points)	A/B x 100 = % (C)
Assignments	[ ]		8	

WEEK 5 AVERAGE	Add up column C and divide by number of included [X] assignments =	%

COURSE PLAN (FIRST QUARTER)
WEEK SIX

LATIN
Grade 3

Weekly Breakdown	Goals and Notes for the Week
Adjectives, proper nouns, common nouns.	Be familiar with defintion of adjectives, nouns, prōnouns. Know the difference between common and proper nouns. Begin learning about Latin personal prōnouns.

Student Daily Assignments	X	Parent Daily Guidelines
DAY 1 **LESSON THREE** Read p. 11 of drillbook. *HOMEWORK: Complete exercises on p. 11 of drillbook. Study p. 9 and 12 of drillbook.	☐ ☐	(NEEDED: Drillbook.) INTRODUCE *"Latin Personal Prōnouns"* on p. 11 of drillbook. EXPLAIN 1st, 2nd and 3rd person. COPY chart of English prōnouns of English prōnouns on board. COMPARE with chart of Latin prōnouns. HAVE students take turns filling in chart on board. *HOMEWORK: Complete exercises on p. 11 of drillbook. Study p. 9 and 12 in drillbook.
DAY 2 Read p. 1 and 9 in drillbook. *HOMEWORK: Study Grammar Questions, p. 2, 6, and True and False on p. 12 in workbook and Vocabulary p. 1, 9 in drillbook. Re-read p. 2-7 in the reader.	☐ ☐	(NEEDED: drillbook) REVIEW vocabulary on p. 1 and 9 in drillbook. MAKE charts on the board of Latin being verbs on p. 6 and have students fill them in. DISCUSS personal prōnouns on p. 11 of drillbook. REVIEW 1st, 2nd, 3rd person and the concepts of "singular" and "plural". *HOMEWORK: Study *Grammar Questions,* p. 2, 6, and *True and False* on p. 12 in workbook and Vocabulary p. 1 and 9 in drillbook. Re-read p. 2-7 in the reader.
DAY 3 Read p. 2-7 in reader. Read p. 2, 6, 12 in workbook. Read p. 4, 8, 12 in drillbook. *HOMEWORK: Complete p. 9-10 in drillbook. Study, prayers, phrase and new saying on p. 12 of drillbok.	☐ ☐	(NEEDED: Drillbook, workbook, reader.) RE-READ all stories in the reader on p. 2-7. REVIEW *"Grammar Questions"* on p. 2, 6, 12 in workbook. HAVE students write on board Latin prayers, phrases and sayings from p. 4, 8, 12 in drillbook. *HOMEWORK: Study *Grammar Questions,* p. 2, 6, 12 in workbook and Vocabulary p. 1, 5, 9 in drillbook. Study new Latin saying on p. 12 in drillbook.
DAY 4 Take Lesson 3 Quiz on p. 48 of the Teacher Guide.	☐	**LESSON THREE QUIZ:** VOCABULARY: New vocabulary, p. 6 of workbook. GRAMMAR: Grammar Questions, p. 6 of workbook. LATIN SAYING: p. 12 of drillbook. **"Tota pulchra es, Maria."**

WEEK SIX Grade Book

ASSIGNMENTS	Include X	(A) Points Earned	(B) Possible Points)	A/B x 100 = % (C)
Lesson Three Quiz	☐		15	
Assignments	☐		6	
WEEK 6 AVERAGE	**Add up column C and divide by number of included X assignments =**			%

Weekly Breakdown		Goals and Notes for the Week
First declension plural nouns, noun endings.		Be familiar with defintion of singular and plural nouns. Students will learn how the plural endings is placed on the roots of Latin first declension nouns.

	Student Daily Assignments	[X]	Parent Daily Guidelines
DAY 1	**LESSON FOUR** Read p. 13-14 in workbook. *HOMEWORK: Complete exercises on p. 13-14 of workbook.	☐ ☐	(NEEDED: Workbook.) **INTRODUCE** *"First Declension Plural Nouns"* and *"New Latin Nouns"* on p. 13 of workbook. **DISCUSS A. Plural Practice** on p. 14. **HAVE** students take turns making first declension plural nouns. **DO C. Pronunciation Practice** on p. 14 in class. *HOMEWORK: Complete exercises on p. 13-14 of workbook.
DAY 2	Read p. 8-9 in reader. Read p. 16 in drillbook. *HOMEWORK: Reread story on p. 8 of reader with audio. Complete exercises on p. 16 of drillbook.	☐ ☐	(NEEDED: Drillbook, reader.) **READ** *"New Words To Learn"* on p. 8 of reader. **HAVE STUDENTS READ** story on p. 9 of reader once without stopping. Read again and ask for translations. Correct as necessary. **INTRODUCE** new *"Ego Sum"* phrase, the next phrase of **Ave Maria** and new Latin saying on p. 16 of drillbook. *HOMEWORK: Reread story on p. 8 of reader with audio. Complete exercises on p. 16 of drillbook.
DAY 3	Read p. 13-14 in drillbook. *HOMEWORK: Reread story with audio. Review **casa, villa, ecclēsia, via, silva,** Complete p. 13-14 in drillbook.	☐ ☐	(NEEDED: Drillbook.) **REVIEW** *"Definitions"* and *"New Vocabulary"* on p. 13 of drillbook. **DISCUSS** *"Latin-English Cognates"* and the use of **familia** on p. 14. **DRAW** the chart on p. 14 on the board and have students fill in missing singular or plural forms of first declension feminine nouns. *HOMEWORK: Reread story with **audio.** Review **casa, villa, ecclēsia, via, silva.** Complete p. 13-14 in drillbook.
DAY 4	Review p. 4, 8, 12, 16 of drillbook. *HOMEWORK: Reread story on p. 9 of reader with audio. Complete exercises on p. 15 of workbook.	☐ ☐	(NEEDED: Teacher's Guide, drillbook.) Do **Lesson Four Boardwork Suggestion**s on p. 78 of Teacher's Guide. **HAVE** students practice writing the **Signum Crucis, Ego Sum** and **Ave Maria** phrases and Latin sayings on the board from p. 4, 8, 12 and 16 of drillbook. *HOMEWORK: Reread story on p. 9 of reader with audio. Complete exercises on p. 15 of workbook.

WEEK SEVEN Grade Book				
ASSIGNMENTS	Include [X]	(A) Points Earned	(B) Possible Points)	A/B x 100 = % (C)
Assignments	☐		8	
WEEK 7 AVERAGE	**Add up column C and divide by number of included [X] assignments =**			%

COURSE PLAN (FIRST QUARTER)

WEEK EIGHT

Weekly Breakdown	Goals and Notes for the Week
First declension plural nouns, noun endings.	Be familiar with defintion of singular and plural nouns. Students will learn how the plural endings is placed on the roots of Latin first declension nouns. More about Latin personal prōnouns.

	Student Daily Assignments	[X]	Parent Daily Guidelines
DAY 1	**LESSON FOUR** Read p. 15-16 in drillbook. *HOMEWORK: Complete p. 15 of drillbook.	☐ ☐	(NEEDED: Drillbook.) **REVIEW** charts on p. 6 and 11. **DISCUSS** p. 16 of drillbook. **WRITE** personal prōnoun phrases from p. 15 on board. **MAKE** chart on p. 14 as time permists. **DISCUSS** *"ID EST"* on p. 15 of drillbook. *HOMEWORK: Complete exercises on p. 15 of drillbook.
DAY 2	Review p. 2, 6, 12 in workbook. Review p. 1, 6, 9, 13 in workbook. *HOMEWORK: Complete exercises on p. 16 of workbook. Study p. 16 of drillbook.	☐ ☐	(NEEDED: Workbook) **READ** *"Grammar Questions"* on p. 2 and 6 and *"True or False"* on p. 12 in workbook and new words on p. 1, 6, 9, 13. of workbook. **DISCUSS** p. 16 in workbook. **COMPLETE G. Subject-Adjective Identification** on p. 16 on board. **REPEAT Boardwork Suggestions** as necessary. *HOMEWORK: Complete exercises on p. 16 of workbook. Study p. 16 of drillbook.
DAY 3	Read p. 8-9 in reader. Read p. 13-16 in drillbook. *HOMEWORK: REVIEW "Definitions" and "New Vocabulary" on p. 1, 5, 9, and 13 in drillbook. REVIEW on the board Latin prayers and sayings on p. 4, 8, 12, and 16 in the drillbook.	☐ ☐	(NEEDED: Drillbook, reader.) **RE-READ** p. 8-9 in reader. **REVIEW** *"Definitions"* and *"New Vocabulary"* on p. 13 and **Nominative Plurals** chart on p. 14 of drillbook. **REVIEW** on the board Latin prayers and sayings on p. 16. *HOMEWORK: REVIEW "Definitions" and "New Vocabulary" on p. 13 in drillbook. REVIEW Latin prayers and sayings on p. 16 in the drillbook.
DAY 4	Lesson 4 Quiz on p. 49 of the **Teacher's Guide**.	☐	**LESSON FOUR QUIZ:** **VOCABULARY:** New vocabulary, p. 13 of drillbook. **NOMINATIVE PLURALS CHART,** p. 14 of drillbook. **LATIN SAYING:** "Viae vestrae nōn sunt viae meae, dicit Dominus." on p. 16 of the drillbook.

WEEK EIGHT Grade Book

ASSIGNMENTS	Include [X]	(A) Points Earned	(B) Possible Points)	A/B x 100 = % (C)
Lesson Four Quiz	☐		14	
Assignments	☐		6	
WEEK 8 AVERAGE		**Add up column C and divide by number of included [X] assignments =**		

WEEK NINE

Weekly Breakdown	Goals and Notes for the Week
Comprehensive review of grammar concepts and vocabulary presented in the first seven weeks.	Review grammar concepts, vocabulary (nouns, adjectives, being verbs, adverbs, conjunctions, prepositions) and practical application for first quarter exam.

Student Daily Assignments	[X]	Parent Daily Guidelines
DAY 1 Review first four lessons in the drillbook. *HOMEWORK: REVIEW the "Definitions" from p. 1, 5, 9 and 13 of the drillbook. REVIEW the phrases, prayers and sayings from p. 4, 8, 12, and 16 in drill-book.	☐ ☐	(**NEEDED:** Drillbook, Teacher's Guide) **REVIEW** sample exercises from the **Boardwork Suggestions** for the first four lessons. **REVIEW** *"Definitions"* from p. 1, 5, 9 and 13 of the drillbook. **REVIEW** the phrases, prayers and sayings from p. 4, 8, 12, and 16 in drillbook. *HOMEWORK: REVIEW *"Definitions"* from p. 1, 5, 9 and 13 of the drillbook. **REVIEW** the phrases, prayers and sayings from p. 4, 8, 12, and 16 in drillbook.
DAY 2 Review p. 17-18 in workbook. *HOMEWORK: Complete all exercises on p. 17-18 in workbook. Re-read stories in reader from p. 1-9.	☐ ☐	(**NEEDED:** Workbook) **DISCUSS A. Grammar Review** and vocabulary reviews on p. 17 in workbook. **WRITE** samples from **Exercises E, F, and G** on p. 18 on board and have students take turns completing them. *HOMEWORK: Complete all exercises on p. 17-18 in workbook.
DAY 3 Read p. 1-9 in reader. Read p. 4, 8, 12, and 16 in the drillbook. *HOMEWORK: Review all exer-cises on p. 17-18 in workbook Study all Latin Sayings from p. 2-16 in drillbook.	☐ ☐	(**NEEDED:** Drillbook, reader, Teacher's Guide) **REVIEW** sample exercises from the **Boardwork Suggestions** from as desired. **RE-READ** stories in reader from p. 1-9. **RE-VIEW** all Latin sayings from p. 4, 8, 12, and 16 in drillbook. *HOMEWORK: Review all exercises on p. 17-18 in workbook Study all Latin Sayings from p. 2-16 in drillbook.
DAY 4 First Quarter Exam on p. 50 of the **Teacher Guide.**	☐	**FIRST QUARTER EXAM**

WEEK NINE Grade Book				
ASSIGNMENTS	Include [X]	(A) Points Earned	(B) Possible Points)	A/B x 100 = % (C)
First Quarter Exam	☐		42	
Assignments	☐		6	
WEEK 9 AVERAGE		**Add up column C and divide by number of included [X] assignments =**		%

COURSE PLAN (FIRST QUARTER)

	Weekly Averages	Weekly Percent Grade (A)	
Record from Week 1 grades →	Week 1 Average		
Record from Week 2 grades →	Week 2 Average		
Record from Week 3 grades →	Week 3 Average		
Record from Week 4 grades →	Week 4 Average		
Record from Week 5 grades →	Week 5 Average		
Record from Week 6 grades →	Week 6 Average		
Record from Week 7 grades →	Week 7 Average		
Record from Week 8 grades →	Week 8 Average		
Record from Week 9 grades →	Week 9 Average		
Sum of Weekly Percent Grades from Column A =		**(B)**	
Total Weekly Grade Average	Divide B/8 =	%	
QUARTER 1 LATIN GRADE	Letter Grade Equivalent (see report card) =		

COURSE PLAN (SECOND QUARTER)

WEEK TEN

Weekly Breakdown	Goals and Notes for the Week
Being verb in present tense, third person singular and plural endings. Conjunction **et**.	Understand the use of the third person plural being verb *sunt (they are)*. Understand the conjunction *et (and)* and compound subjects.

	Student Daily Assignments [X]		Parent Daily Guidelines
DAY 1	**LESSON FIVE** Read p. 19-20 in workbook. *HOMEWORK: Complete p. 19-20 in workbook.	☐ ☐	(**NEEDED:** Workbook.) **INTRODUCE** *"The Being Verb Sunt"* and *"Being Verbs"* on p. 19 of workbook. **WRITE A. Latin Practice** on p. 20 on board and complete with class. **DISCUSS** examples of compound subjects on p. 20 in **B. Name the Picture. EXPLAIN** the use of the third person plural being verb **sunt** with plural subjects and compound subjects joined by the conjunction *et*. *HOMEWORK: Complete p. 19-20 in workbook.
DAY 2	Read p. 10-11 in reader. Read p. 20 in drillbook. *HOMEWORK: Re-read story with onine **audio**. Complete exercises on p. 20 of drillbook. Read p. 10-11 in reader.	☐ ☐	(**NEEDED:** Drillbook, reader.) **READ** *"New Words To Learn"* on p. 10 of reader. **HAVE STUDENTS READ** story on p. 11 of reader without stopping. **READ** again and ask for translations. Correct as necessary. **INTRODUCE** the new **Ego Sum** phrase, next phrase of **Ave Maria** and new Latin saying on p. 20 of drillbook. **HOMEWORK:** Re-read story with online **audio**. Complete exercises on p. 20 of drillbook.
DAY 3	Read p. 9-10 of drillbook. *HOMEWORK: Complete p. 17-18 of drillbook. Reread story on p. 11 in reader with **audio**. Review **nōn, sunt, et.** Review Week 5 Saying on p. 20 in drillbook.	☐ ☐	(**NEEDED:** Drillbook.) **DISCUSS** *"Definitions"* and *"New Vocabulary"* and the conjunction **"et"** on p. 17 of drillbook. **READ** *"The Ampersand"* on p. 19 of drillbook. **DO** *"Using Being Verbs"* on p. 18 on the board. *HOMEWORK: Complete p. 17-18 of drillbook. Reread story on p. 11 in reader with **audio**. Review **nōn, sunt, et.** Review Week 5 Saying on p. 20 in drillbook.
DAY 4	Read p. 21 in workbook. *HOMEWORK: Complete p. 21-22 of workbook.	☐ ☐	(**NEEDED:** Teacher's Guide.) **WORK** through **Boardwork Suggestions** in the Teacher's Guide on p. 79 with the class. **DISCUSS** *"Plural Subjects"* on p. 21 in workbook and **F. Parts of Speech** on p. 22 of workbook. *HOMEWORK: Complete p. 21-22 of workbook.

WEEK TEN Grade Book				
ASSIGNMENTS	Include [X]	(A) Points Earned	(B) Possible Points)	A/B x 100 = % (C)
Assignments	☐		8	
WEEK 10 AVERAGE	Add up column C and divide by number of included [X] assignments =			%

WEEK ELEVEN

Weekly Breakdown	Goals and Notes for the Week
Being verb in present tense, third person singular and plural endings. Conjunction **et**.	Understand the use of the third person plural being verb *sunt (they are)*. Understand the conjunction *et (and)* and compound subjects.

	Student Daily Assignments	[X]	Parent Daily Guidelines
DAY 1	**LESSON FIVE** Read p. 19 in drillbook. *HOMEWORK: Complete the exercises on p. 19 in drillbook and study Latin prayer, phrase and saying on p. 20 of drillbook.	☐ ☐	(NEEDED: Drillbook.) **REVIEW** charts on p. 19 of drillbook. **HAVE** students practice making charts on the board. *HOMEWORK: Complete p. 19 in drillbook and study Latin prayer, phrase and saying on p. 20 of drillbook.
DAY 2	Read p. 22 of workbook. *HOMEWORK: Complete exercises on p. 21-22 of workbook.	☐ ☐	(NEEDED: Workbook) **DISCUSS E. Subject/Predicate Adjectives** on p. 22 of workbook with class. **WRITE** the 5 parts of speech used in **F. Parts of Speech** on p. 22 on board and have students classify the Latin words. **SHOW** students how to compose sentences in **G. English-to-Latin** on p. 22. HOMEWORK: Complete exercises on p. 21-22 of workbook.
DAY 3	Read p. 10-11 in reader. Read p. 17 of drillbook. *HOMEWORK: Reread story on p. 11 in reader with **audio**. Review **nōn, sunt, et.** Review Week 5 Saying on p. 20 in drillbook.	☐ ☐	(NEEDED: Drillbook, reader.) **REVIEW** *"Definitions"* and *"New Vocabulary"* on p. 17 of drillbook. **RE-READ** story on p. 11 in reader. **HAVE** students write new prayers, phrase and saying from p. 20 of drillbook on the board. *HOMEWORK: Reread story on p. 11 in reader with **audio**. Review **nōn, sunt, et.** Review Week 5 Saying on p. 20 in drillbook.
DAY 4	Lesson 5 Quiz on p. 52 of the Teacher's Guide.	☐	**LESSON FIVE QUIZ:** **VOCABULARY:** New vocabulary: **nōn, est, sunt, et.** **USING EST AND SUNT:** 5 sentences from p. 22 of drillbook for students to translate. **LATIN SAYING:** "**Sunt septem ecclēsiæ in Asiā.**"

WEEK ELEVEN Grade Book				
ASSIGNMENTS	Include [X]	(A) Points Earned	(B) Possible Points)	A/B x 100 = % (C)
Lesson Five Quiz	☐		10	
Assignments	☐		6	
WEEK 11 AVERAGE	Add up column C and divide by number of included [X] assignments =			%

Weekly Breakdown	Goals and Notes for the Week
Adjectives of quality, and the adverb **nōn**.	Understand the position of Latin adjectives of quality which answer the question "what kind?" Adjectives of quality usually come after the nouns they modify.

	Student Daily Assignments	[X]	Parent Daily Guidelines
DAY 1	**LESSON SIX** Read p. 23 in workbook. ***HOMEWORK:** Complete p. 23-24 of workbook. Review 6 new adjectives. **bona, parva, opulenta, pulchra, Christiāna, Rōmāna.**	☐ ☐	(**NEEDED:** Workbook.) **READ** p. 23 in workbook aloud, explaining that Latin adjectives of quality answer the question "what kind" and follow the nouns they modify. **WRITE** definition of "adjective of quality" on board. **COMPLETE A. Adjective Practice** on p. 23 of workbook. **REVIEW** 6 adjectives: **bona, parva, opulenta, pulchra, Christiāna, Rōmāna.** ***HOMEWORK:** Complete p. 23-24 of workbook.
DAY 2	Read p. 12-13 in reader. Read p. 24 in drillbook. ***HOMEWORK:** Reread story on p. 12-13 of reader with online **audio.** Complete p. 24 of drillbook.	☐ ☐	(**NEEDED:** Reader, drillbook.) **READ** *"New Words To Learn"* on p. 12 of **reader** with students. **HAVE STUDENTS READ** story on p. 13 of **reader** once without stopping. Read each sentence again and ask for translations. Correct as necessary. **DISCUSS** new **Ego Sum** phrase, new phrase of **Ave Maria** and Week 6 Latin saying on p. 24 of drillbook. ***HOMEWORK:** Reread story on p. 12-13 of reader with online **audio.** Complete p. 24 of drillbook.
DAY 3	Read p. 21-22 in drillbook. ***HOMEWORK:** Complete p. 21-22 of drillbook.. Reread story on p. 13 of reader. Review 6 adjectives: **bona, parva, opulenta, pulchra, Christiāna, Rōmāna.** Review "adjectives of quality and quantity".	☐ ☐	(**NEEDED:** Drillbook.) **DISCUSS** *"Definitions"* and *"The Adverb Non"* on p. 21 of drillbook. **DO** the exercises in *"Adjectives of Quality"* on p. 22 of drillbook on the board with the class. ***HOMEWORK:** Complete p. 21-22 of drillbook. Reread story on p. 13 of reader. Review 6 adjectives: **bona, parva, opulenta, pulchra, Christiāna, Rōmāna.** Review "adjectives of quality and quantity"
DAY 4	Read p. 25 in workbook. ***HOMEWORK:** Complete the exercises on p. 25 in workbook.	☐ ☐	(**NEEDED:** Teacher's Guide, workbook.) **DO** the **Boardwork Suggestions** on p. 79 on board with the class. Do exercises on p. 25 in the workbook as desired. ***HOMEWORK:** Complete exercises on p. 25 in workbook.

WEEK TWELVE Grade Book

ASSIGNMENTS	Include [X]	(A) Points Earned	(B) Possible Points	A/B x 100 = % (C)
Assignments	☐		8	
WEEK 12 AVERAGE	**Add up column C and divide by number of included [X] assignments =**			%

COURSE PLAN (SECOND QUARTER)
WEEK THIRTEEN

8	Weekly Breakdown	Goals and Notes for the Week
	Adjectives of quality, and the adverb **nōn**.	Understand the position of Latin adjectives of quality which answer the question "what kind?". Adjectives of quality usually come after the nouns they modify.

	Student Daily Assignments	[X]	Parent Daily Guidelines
DAY 1	**LESSON SIX** Read p. 23 in drillbook. *HOMEWORK: Complete p. 23 of drillbook. Study the Latin phrases, prayers and Lesson 6 Saying on p. 24.	☐ ☐	(NEEDED: Drillbook.) **INTRODUCE** *"Adjectives of Quantiity"* on p. 23 in drillbook. **WRITE** the ten cardinal number phrases on board. **HAVE** students practice writing cardinal number phrases with the nouns **femina, via, ancilla**. *HOMEWORK: Complete p. 23 of drillbook. Study the Latin phrases, prayers and Lesson 6 Saying on p. 24.
DAY 2	Read p. 23 and 26 in workbook. *HOMEWORK: Complete p. 26 in workbook.	☐ ☐	(NEEDED: Workbook, Teacher's Guide.) **REVIEW** "adjectives of quality" on p. 23 in workbook. **REVIEW** 6 adjectives on p. 9 of workbook. **DO** exercises on p. 26 of workbook with class and **Boardwork Suggestions** on p. 79 of Teacher's Guide as needed. *HOMEWORK: Complete p. 26 in workbook.
DAY 3	Read p. 12-13 in reader. Read p. 17 and 21 in drillbook. *HOMEWORK: Review p. 17 nd 21 in drillbook. Reread story on p. 13 of reader. Review 6 adjectives: **bona, parva, opulenta, pulchra, Christiāna, Rōmāna**. Review "adjectives of quality and quantity". Study the Latin phrases, prayers and Lesson 6 Saying on p. 24 of drillbook.	☐ ☐	(NEEDED: Drillbook reader.) **RE-READ** p. 12-13 in reader. **REVIEW** *"Definitions"* on p. 17 and 21 in drillbook. **REVIEW** adjectives and Latin phrase, prayer and Lesson 6 Saying on the board. **HAVE** students write the phrase, prayer and saying on p. 24 in drillbook on the board. *HOMEWORK: Review p. 17 and 21 in drillbook. Reread story on p. 13 of reader. Review 6 adjectives: **bona, parva, opulenta, pulchra, Christiāna, Rōmāna**. Review "adjectives of quality and quantity". Study the Latin phrases, prayers and Lesson 6 Saying on p. 24 of drillbook.
DAY 4	Take Lesson 6 Quiz on p. 53 of **Teacher s Guide.**	☐	**LESSON SIX QUIZ:** **VOCABULARY: bona, parva, opulenta, pulchra, Christiāna, Rōmāna.** **ADJECTIVES OF QUALITY:** 5 sentences from p. 24 of workbook. **LATIN SAYING:** "Pulchra es et decora, filia Jerusalem."

WEEK THIRTEEN Grade Book

ASSIGNMENTS	Include [X]	(A) Points Earned	(B) Possible Points	A/B x 100 = % (C)
Lesson Six Quiz	☐		12	
Assignments	☐		6	
WEEK 13 AVERAGE		Add up column C and divide by number of included [X] assignments =		

COURSE PLAN (SECOND QUARTER)

LATIN
Grade 3

WEEK FOURTEEN

Weekly Breakdown	Goals and Notes for the Week
The preposition **in** and prepositional phrases. Singular objects of the preposition in often end in -ā.	Understand that prepositions show relationships between words in a sentence. Singular objects of the preposition **in** are nouns which use the singular ablative ending -ā.

Student Daily Assignments	X	Parent Daily Guidelines
DAY 1 **LESSON SEVEN** Read p. 27 in workbook. ☐ ***HOMEWORK:** Complete p. 27-28 of workbook. ☐		(**NEEDED:** Workbook.) **READ** p. 27 in workbook aloud, explaining the function of prepositions. **SHOW** how the singular object of the preposition **in** takes the singlar ablative ending -ā. **WRITE** the 5 prepositional phrases on the board. **DISCUSS A. Grammar Practice** on p. 27. ***HOMEWORK:** Complete p. 27-28 of workbook.
DAY 2 Read p. 14-17 in reader. Read p. 28 in drillbook. ☐ ***HOMEWORK:** Reread stories on p. 14-17 with **audio**. Complete exercises on p. 14 of **drillbook**. Learn Week 7 Latin Saying. "**Confitēbor tibi in ecclēsiā magnā.**" ☐		(**NEEDED:** Drillbook, reader.) **READ** "New Words To Learn" on p. 14 of reader with students. **HAVE** students take turns reading p. 15-17 in reader aloud in class. **INTRODUCE** the new **Ego Sum phrase**, the **Ave Maria phrase** and the Week 7 Latin saying on p. 28 in drillbook. ***HOMEWORK:** Reread p. 14-17 in reader with **audio**. Complete exercises on p. 28 of drillbook. Learn Week 7 Latin Saying. "**Confitēbor tibi in ecclēsiā magnā.**"
DAY 3 Read p. 25 and 27 in drillbook. ☐ ***HOMEWORK:** Complete p. 25 and 27 of drillbook. ☐		(**NEEDED:** Drillbook.) **INTRODUCE** the *"Definitions"* on p. 25 of drillbook. **DO** the *"New Prepositional Phrases"* on p. 25 of drillbook. **SHOW** class on board how to bracket prepositional phrases in exercises on p. 27 of drillbook. ***HOMEWORK:** Complete p. 25 and 27 of drillbook.
DAY 4 Read p. 29 in workbook. ☐ ***HOMEWORK:** Complete p. 29 of workbook. ☐		(**NEEDED:** Teacher's Guide, workbook.) **DO** the **Lesson Seven Boardwork Suggestions** on p. 79 of the Teacher's Guide with the class on the board. **DO** the exercises on p. 29 of the workbook with the class on the board. ***HOMEWORK:** Complete p. 29 of workbook.

WEEK FOURTEEN Grade Book

ASSIGNMENTS	Include X	(A) Points Earned	(B) Possible Points	A/B x 100 = % (C)
Assignments	☐		8	
WEEK 14 AVERAGE		**Add up column C and divide by number of included X assignments =**		%

19

COURSE PLAN (SECOND QUARTER)

WEEK FIFTEEN

Weekly Breakdown	Goals and Notes for the Week
The preposition **in** and prepositional phrases. Singular objects of the preposition in often end in -ā.	Understand that prepositions show relationships between words in a sentence. Singular objects of the preposition **in** are nouns which use the singular ablative ending -ā.

Student Daily Assignments [X]	Parent Daily Guidelines
DAY 1 **LESSON SEVEN** Read p. 26 of drillbook. *HOMEWORK: Complete p. 26 of drillbook. Study Latin phrases and sayings on p. 28 of drillbook.	☐ **(NEEDED: Drillbook.)** READ *"First Declension Endings"* on p. 26 of drillbook. **WRITE** the five singular endings on the board first, and then the 5 plural endings. **WRITE** the declension of **ecclesia** as shown on the board. **HAVE** class take turns copying it on board. **DECLINE silva** in the same manner, singular endings first. ☐ *HOMEWORK: Complete p. 26 of drillbook. Study Latin phrases and sayings on p. 28 of drillbook.
DAY 2 Read p. 30 in the workbook. *HOMEWORK: Complete exercises on p. 30 of workbook.	☐ **(NEEDED: Workbook, Teacher Guide.)** **REPEAT** the **Boardwork Suggestions** for Lesson 7 on p. 79 of Teacher's Guide as needed. **WRITE** chart on p. 30 in workbook on the board. **HAVE** students fill in the chart. ☐ *HOMEWORK: Complete exercises on p. 30 of workbook.
DAY 3 Read p. 14-17 in reader. Read p. 27 in workbook. *HOMEWORK: Reread story with **audio**. Complete Grammar Review on p. 27 of workbook. Review prepositional phases on p. 17 of workbook. Review phrase, prayer and Week 7 Latin Saying on p. 28 in drillbook.	☐ **(NEEDED: Workbook, reader, drillbook.)** **RE-READ** p. 14-17 in reader. **REVIEW** the adjectives and nouns on p. 17 in workbook and write on the board 5 prepositional phrases on p. 27 of the workbook. **HAVE** students write Latin phrase, prayer and saying from p. 28 of drillbook on the board. ☐ *HOMEWORK: Reread story with **audio**. Complete Grammar Review on p. 27 of workbook. Review the prepositional phases on p. 17 of workbook. Review phrase, prayer and Week 7 Latin Saying on p. 28 in drillbook.
DAY 4 Lesson 7 Quiz on p. 54 of the **Teacher Guide.**	☐ **LESSON SEVEN QUIZ:** **5 PREPOSITIONAL PHRASES:** (on p. 27 of workbook.) **GRAMMAR REVIEW** (Sentences from p. 27 of drillbook.) **LATIN SAYING:** "Confitēbor tibi, etc." p. 28, drillbook.

WEEK FIFTEEN Grade Book

ASSIGNMENTS	Include [X]	(A) Points Earned	(B) Possible Points	A/B x 100 = % (C
Lesson Seven Quiz	☐		18	
Assignments	☐		6	
WEEK 15 AVERAGE	**Add up column C and divide by number of included** [X] **assignments =**			%

COURSE PLAN (SECOND QUARTER)
WEEK SIXTEEN

Weekly Breakdown	Goals and Notes for the Week
Plural adjective phrases, new preposiiton **ad**, new adjectives and new verbs.	Understand how adjectives must agree with nouns they modify in case, number and gender. Learn the new preposition **ad** and the accusative singular ending -**am**. Learn 3 intransitive verbs.

Student Daily Assignments	[X]	Parent Daily Guidelines
DAY 1 **LESSON EIGHT** Read p. 31-32 in the workbook. *HOMEWORK: Complete p. 31-32 of workbook.	☐ ☐	(**NEEDED**: Workbook) **READ** *"Modifying Nouns"* on p. 31 in workbook. **WRITE** the 4 adjectives on p. 31 on board and have class take turns writing them. **READ** *"The Preposition Ad"* and 4 new prepositional phrases. **READ** *"New Intransitive Verbs"* on p. 32. **DO A. Intransitive Verb Practice** on board with class. *HOMEWORK: Complete p. 31-32 in workbook.
DAY 2 Read p. 18-21 in reader. Read p. 15-16 in workbook. *HOMEWORK: Re-read p. 18-21 with online **audio** in reader. Complete p. 32 in drillbook.	☐ ☐	(**NEEDED**: Drillbook, reader.) **INTRODUCE** *"New Words To Learn"* on p. 18 of reader. **READ** p. 19-21 in reader with class. **INTRODUCE** the new **Ego Sum** phrase, the last phrase of the **Ave Maria** and Lesson 8 Latin Saying on p. 32 of drillbook. *HOMEWORK: Re-read p. 18-21 with online **audio** in reader. Complete p. 32 in drillbook.
DAY 3 Read p. 29-30 in drillbook. *HOMEWORK: Complete p. 29 and "New Prepositional Phrases" on p. 30 of drillbook. Study phrase, prayer and Lesson 8 Latin Saying on p. 32 of drillbook.	☐ ☐	(**NEEDED**: Drillbook.) **READ** the *"Definitions"* and the *"New Vocabulary"* on p. 29 of the drillbook. **DISCUSS** the *"Latin-English Cognates"* on p. 29 of drillbook and the sections on **magnanimous** and the first conjugation verb **cantō**, on p. 30 of drillbook. *HOMEWORK: Complete p. 29 and "New Prepositional Phrases" on p. 30 of drillbook. Study phrase, prayer and Lesson 8 Latin Saying on p. 32 of drillbook.
DAY 4 Read p. 33 in workbook. *HOMEWORK: Complete p. 33 in workbook.	☐ ☐	(**NEEDED**: Teacher's Guide, workbook.) **DO** the **Lesson 8 Boardwork Suggestions** on p. 80 of Teacher's Guide. **EXPLAIN** Exercises D, E, F on p. 33 of workbook on the board with class as time permits. *HOMEWORK: Complete p. 33 in workbook.

WEEK SIXTEEN Grade Book				
ASSIGNMENTS	Include [X]	(A) Points Earned	(B) Possible Points)	A/B x 100 = % (C)
Assignments	☐		8	
WEEK 16 AVERAGE		**Add up column C and divide by number of included [X] assignments =**		**%**

COURSE PLAN (SECOND QUARTER)
WEEK SEVENTEEN

LATIN
Grade 3

Weekly Breakdown	Goals and Notes for the Week
Plural adjective phrases, new preposiiton **ad**, new adjectives and new verbs.	Understand how adjectives must agree with nouns they modify in case, number and gender. Learn the new preposition **ad** and the accusative singular ending **-am**. Learn 3 intransitive verbs.

	Student Daily Assignments [X]	Parent Daily Guidelines
DAY 1	**LESSON EIGHT** Read p. 30-31 in the drillbook. *HOMEWORK: Complete p. 30-31 of drillbook. Study Latin saying on p. 32: **"Cantātē Dominō canticum novum."**	(NEEDED: Drillbook.) **READ** *"First Conjugation Verbs"* on p. 30 of drillbook with class. **DRAW** chart of first conjugation personal endings on p. 30-31 on board, singular endings first, then plural. **HAVE** students fill in charts. **DO** "First Conjugation Verb Matching" on p. 31 with class on board. *HOMEWORK: Complete p. 30-31 of the drillbook. Study Latin saying on p. 32 of drillbook: **"Cantāte Dominō canticum novum."**
DAY 2	Read p. 18-21 in reader. Read p. 33-34 in workbook. *HOMEWORK: Complete p. 34 in workbook. Review new adjectives, verbs and prepositional phrases on p. 31-32 of workbook.	(NEEDED: Workbook, Teacher's Guide.) **REPEAT** Lesson 8 Boardwork Suggestions on p. 80 of the Teacher's Guide as needed. **DO** exercises on p. 33-34 of the workbook on board with class as needed. **REVIEW** new adjectives, verbs and prepositional phrases on p. 31-32 in worbook. *HOMEWORK: Complete p. 34 in workbook. Review new adjectives, verbs and prepositional phrases on p. 31-32 of workbook.
DAY 3	Read p. 18-21 in reader. Read p. 29-30 in drillbook. *HOMEWORK: Read p. 18-21 in reader with **audio**. Review the "Definitions" and "New Vocabulary" on p. 29 and prepositional phrases on p. 30 of drillbook. Study Latin saying, on p. 32.	(NEEDED: Drillbook, reader.) **RE-READ** p. 18-21 in the reader. **REVIEW** the *"Definitions"* and "**New Vocabulary**" on p. 29 and prepositional phrases on p. 30 of drillbook. **HAVE** students write Latin prayers, phrases and sayings from p. 20, 24, 28 and 32 of drillbook on board. *HOMEWORK: Read p. 18-21 in the reader with online **audio**. Review the "Definitions" and "New Vocabulary" on p. 29 and prepositional phrases on p. 30 of drillbook. Study Latin saying, on p. 32.
DAY 4	Take Lesson 8 Quiz on p. 55 of **Teacher Guide.**	**LESSON EIGHT QUIZ:** **PREPOSITIONAL PHRASES:** on p. 31 of workbook. **NEW VOCABULARY: magna, parva, antīqua, longa, splendida, ambulat, cantat, ōrat.** **LATIN SAYING:** "Cantāte Dominō, etc." p. 32, drillbook.

WEEK SEVENTEEN Grade Book

ASSIGNMENTS	Include [X]	(A) Points Earned	(B) Possible Points)	A/B x 100 = % (C)
Lesson Eight Quiz	☐		12	
Assignments	☐		6	
WEEK 17 AVERAGE		Add up column C and divide by number of included [X] assignments =		%

COURSE PLAN (SECOND QUARTER)

LATIN
Grade 3

WEEK EIGHTEEN

Weekly Breakdown	Goals and Notes for the Week
Comprehensive review of grammar concepts and vocabulary presented in Weeks 10-17.	Review grammar concepts, vocabulary (nouns, adjectives, being verbs, adverbs, conjunctions, prepositions) and practical application for second quarter exam.

Student Daily Assignments [X]		Parent Daily Guidelines
DAY 1 — Review Lessons 5-8 in the drillbook. *HOMEWORK: Review "Definitions" from p. 17, 21, 25 and 29 of the drillbook. Review the phrases, prayers and sayings from p. 20, 24, 28 and 32 in drillbook.	☐ ☐	(**NEEDED:** Drillbook, Teacher's Guide) **REVIEW** sample exercises from the **Boardwork Suggestions** for Lessons 5-8 on p. 79-80. **REVIEW** *"Definitions"* from p. 17, 21, 25 and 29 of the drillbook. **REVIEW** the phrases, prayers and sayings from p. 20, 24, 28 and 32 in drillbook. *HOMEWORK: Review "Definitions" from p. 17, 21, 25 and 29 of drillbook. Review the phrases, prayers and sayings from p. 20, 24, 28, and 32 in drillbook.
DAY 2 — Review p. 27, 29, 33 and 34 in workbook. *HOMEWORK: Complete all exercises on p. 35-36 in workbook.	☐ ☐	(**NEEDED:** Workbook.) **DISCUSS A. Grammar Review** on p. 27 in workbook. **REVIEW** the **Exercise F. Parts of Speech** on p. 29 and **Exercise H** on p. 34 of workbook on board. **DO** exercises on p. 33 of workbook on board. *HOMEWORK: Complete exercises on p. 35-36 in workbook.
DAY 3 — Read p. 10-21 in reader. Read p. 37-38 in workbook *HOMEWORK: Complete p. 37-38 in workbook. Review p. 35 and 36 in workbook. Study all Latin sayings in drillbook from p. 20, 24, 28, and 32.	☐ ☐	(**NEEDED:** Workbook, reader.) **REVIEW** p. 10-21 in reader. **REVIEW** p. 37-38 in workbook on board with class. **HAVE** class take turns writing Latin sayings from p. 20, 24, 28, and 32 on the board. *HOMEWORK: Complete p. 37-38 in workbook. Review p. 35 and 36 in workbook. Study all Latin sayings in drillbook from p. 20, 24, 28, and 32.
DAY 4 — Second Quarter Exam on p. 56 of the **Teacher's Guide.**	☐	**SECOND QUARTER EXAM**

WEEK EIGHTEEN Grade Book				
ASSIGNMENTS	Include [X]	(A) Points Earned	(B) Possible Points)	A/B x 100 = % (C)
Second Quarter Exam	☐		65	
Assignments	☐		6	
WEEK 18 AVERAGE		Add up column C and divide by number of included [X] assignments =		%

23

COURSE PLAN (SECOND QUARTER)

	Weekly Averages	Weekly Percent Grade (A)	
Record from Week 10 grades →	Week 10 Average		
Record from Week 11 grades →	Week 11 Average		
Record from Week 12 grades →	Week 12 Average		
Record from Week 13 grades →	Week 13 Average		
Record from Week 14 grades →	Week 14 Average		
Record from Week 15 grades →	Week 15 Average		
Record from Week 16 grades →	Week 16 Average		
Record from Week 17 grades →	Week 17 Average		
Record from Week 18 grades →	Week 18 Average		
Sum of Weekly Percent Grades from Column A =		(B)	
Total Weekly Grade Average	Divide B/8 =	%	
QUARTER 2 LATIN GRADE	Letter Grade Equivalent (see report card) =		

24

COURSE PLAN (THIRD QUARTER)
WEEK NINETEEN

Weekly Breakdown	Goals and Notes for the Week
Third person singular verbs, subject-verb agreement, and new verbs and adjectives.	Understand the person and number indicated by the verb ending **-t**. Learn about present tense and learn how subjects must agree with verbs in number. Learn new vocabulary.

Student Daily Assignments	[X]	Parent Daily Guidelines
DAY 1 **LESSON NINE** Read p. 39-40 in workbook. *HOMEWORK: Complete p. 39-40 in workbook.	☐ ☐	(**NEEDED:** Workbook.) **READ** *"Third Person Singular Verbs"* and *"Subject-Verb Agreement"* on p. 39 in workbook with class. **WRITE** the 3 sentences on board and have children translate. **DO A. Subject-Verb Agreement** on p. 40 on board. **INTRODUCE** new nouns and vebs on p. 39. *HOMEWORK: Complete p. 39-40 in workbook.
DAY 2 Read p. 22-23 in reader. Read p. 36 in drillbook. *HOMEWORK: Reread p. 22-23 in reader with online **audio**. Complete exercises on p. 36 of drillbook.	☐ ☐	(**NEEDED:** Drillbook, reader.) **READ** *"New Words To Learn"* on p. 22 and story on p. 23 of reader. Read each sentence again and ask for translations. Correct as necessary. **INTRODUCE** the new **Ego Sum** phrase, next part of the **Ave Maria** and the **Lesson 9 Latin Saying** on p. 36 of drillbook. *HOMEWORK: Reread p. 22-23 in reader with online **audio**. Complete exercises on p. 36 of drillbook.
DAY 3 Read p. 33-34 in drillbook. HOMEWORK: Complete p. 33 and the first half of p. 34 in the drillbook.	☐ ☐	(**NEEDED:** Drillbook.) **READ** the *"Definitions"* and *"New Vocabulary"* on p. 33 in drillbook with class. **EXPLAIN** the *"Latin-English Cognates"* on p. 34. **DO** the *"Latin Antonyms"* on p. 34 with class on the board. *HOMEWORK: Complete p. 33 and the first half of p. 34 in the drillbook
DAY 4 Read p. 41 in workbook. HOMEWORK: Complete p. 41 in workbook.	☐ ☐	(**NEEDED:** Teacher's Guide.) **DO** the **Lesson 9 Boardwork Suggestions** on p. 81 of Teacher's Guide. **DO Exercises D and E** on p. 41 of workbook on the board. *HOMEWORK: Complete p. 41 of workbook.

WEEK NINETEEN Grade Book				
ASSIGNMENTS	Include [X]	(A) Points Earned	(B) Possible Points)	A/B x 100 = % (C)
Assignments	☐		8	
WEEK 19 AVERAGE		Add up column C and divide by number of included [X] assignments =		%

COURSE PLAN (THIRD QUARTER)

LATIN
Grade 3

WEEK TWENTY

Weekly Breakdown	Goals and Notes for the Week
Third person singular verbs, subject-verb agreement, and new verbs and adjectives.	Understand the person and number indicated by the verb ending **-t.** Learn about present tense and learn how subjects must agree with verbs in number. Learn new vocabulary.

Student Daily Assignments	X	Parent Daily Guidelines
DAY 1 **LESSON NINE** Read p. 34-35 in drillbook. *HOMEWORK: Complete p. 34-35 in drillbook. Study new Latin saying on p. 36 of drillbook.	☐ ☐	(**NEEDED:** Drillbook.) **READ** *"More First Conjugation Verbs"* on p. 34 and 35 of drillbook. **MAKE** charts of first conjugation verbs on board and have class fill them in, singular endings first, then plural endings. **HELP** students do exercises on p. 35. *HOMEWORK: Complete p. 34-35 in drillbook. Study new Latin saying on p. 36 of drillbook.
DAY 2 Read p. 41-42 in workbook. *HOMEWORK: Complete p. 41-42 in workbook.	☐ ☐	(**NEEDED:** Workbook, Teacher's Guide.) **DO** the **Lesson 9 Boardwork Suggestions** on p. 81 of the Teacher's Guide with class. **REPEAT** on the board **Exercises D and E** on p. 41 in workbook and **Exercises G and H** on p. 42 if desired.. *HOMEWORK: Complete p. 41-42 in workbook.
DAY 3 Read p. 33-34 in the drillbook. *HOMEWORK: Review definitions and vocabulary on p. 33 and study the Lesson 9 Latin Saying on p. 36 of the drillbook.	☐ ☐	(**NEEDED:** Drillbook, reader.) **RE-READ** p. 22-23 in reader. **REVIEW** the *"Definitions"* and *"New Vocabulary"* on p. 33 of drillbook on board. **HAVE** students write the **Ego Sum** phrases, prayers and Latin sayings on p. 32 and 36 on board. *HOMEWORK: Review definitions and vocabulary on p. 33 and study the Lesson 9 Latin Saying on p. 36 of the drillbook.
DAY 4 Take Lesson 9 Weekly Quiz on p. 59 of the Teacher's Guide	☐	**LESSON NINE QUIZ:** **VOCABULARY: aquila, familia, Nova, recta, saltat, vōltat** **SUBJECT-VERB AGREEMENT:** 5 sentences from **A. Subject-Verb Agreement** on p. 40 of workbook **LATIN SAYING:** "Quī ambulat simpliciter, ambulat confidenter."

WEEK TWENTY Grade Book

ASSIGNMENTS	Include X	(A) Points Earned	(B) Possible Points)	A/B x 100 = % (C)
Lesson Nine Quiz	☐		13	
Assignments	☐		6	
WEEK 20 AVERAGE	Add up column C and divide by number of included X assignments =			

Weekly Breakdown	Goals and Notes for the Week
Third person plural verbs, subject-verb agreement, and new verbs and adjectives.	Understand the person and number indicated by the verb ending **-nt**. Learn how plural subjects must agree with verbs in number. Learn new vocabulary.

	Student Daily Assignments [X]	Parent Daily Guidelines
DAY 1	**LESSON TEN** Read p. 43-44 in workbook. *HOMEWORK: Complete p. 43-44 in workbook.	(NEEDED: Workbook.) ☐ **READ** *"Third Person Singular Verbs"* on p. 43 and explain the third person plural **-nt** ending. **WRITE** the 4 new intransitive verbs on the board. **READ** *"Subject-Verb Agreement"* on p. 43 and write the sentences on the board. **INTRODUCE** new adjectives, nouns on p. 43-44. **DO** Exercises C and D on p. 44 on the board with class. ☐ *HOMEWORK: Complete p. 43-44 in workbook.
DAY 2	Read p. 24-27 in reader. *HOMEWORK: Reread p. 24-27 in reader with online audio. Complete the exercises on p. 40 of drillbook.	(NEEDED: Drillbook, reader.) ☐ **READ** *"New Words To Learn"* on p. 24 and p. 25-27 of reader. **READ** next **Ego Sum** phrase and second half of the **Ave Maria**. **INTRODUCE** new Lesson 10 Latin saying on p. 40 of drillbook. ☐ *HOMEWORK: Reread p. 24-27 in reader with online audio. Complete exercises on p. 40 of drillbook.
DAY 3	Read p. 37-38 in drillbook. *HOMEWORK: Complete p. 37-38 in drillbook. Re-read p. 24-27 in reader. Study Latin saying on p. 40 of drillbook.	(NEEDED: Drillbook.) ☐ **READ** *"Definitions"* and *"New Vocabulary"* on p. 37 of drillbook. **WRITE** the English cognates in *"Latin-English Cognates"* p. 37 on board and help students find related Latin words. **HELP** students with exercise on p. 38 of drillbook as time permits. ☐ *HOMEWORK: Complete p. 37-38 in drillbook. Re-read p. 24-27 in reader. Study Latin saying on p. 40 of drillbook.
DAY 4	Read p. 45 in workbook. *HOMEWORK: Complete p. 45 in workbook.	(NEEDED: Teacher's Guide, workbook.) ☐ **DO** the **Lesson 10 Boardwork Suggestions** on p. 81 in Teacher's Guide. **DO B. Grammar Questions** on p. 44 of workbook. **DO Exercises F and G** on p. 45 of workbook on the board. ☐ *HOMEWORK: Complete p. 45 in workbook.

WEEK TWENTY-ONE Grade Book				
ASSIGNMENTS	Include [X]	(A) Points Earned	(B) Possible Points	A/B x 100 = % (C)
Assignments	☐		8	
WEEK 21 AVERAGE	Add up column C and divide by number of included [X] assignments =			%

Weekly Breakdown	Goals and Notes for the Week
Third person plural verbs, subject-verb agreement, and new verbs and adjectives.	Understand the person and number indicated by the verb ending -**nt**. Learn how plural subjects must agree with verbs in number. Learn new vocabulary.

	Student Daily Assignments	[X]	Parent Daily Guidelines
DAY 1	**LESSON TEN** Read p. 39 in drillbook. *HOMEWORK: Complete p. 39 of drillbook. Study phrase, prayer, and Lesson 10 saying on p. 40 of drillbook: **"Christus ōrat prō nōbīs ut sacerdos."**	☐ ☐	(**NEEDED:** Drillbook.) **READ** *"More First Conjugation Verbs"* on p. 39 of drillbook. **WRITE** charts on p. 39 on board. **HAVE** students fill in singular endings first, then plural endings. **DO** *"Verb Identification"* on p. 39 on board. *HOMEWORK: Complete p. 39 of drillbook. Study phrase, prayer, and Lesson 10 saying on p. 40 of drillbook: **"Christus ōrat prō nōbīs ut sacerdos."**
DAY 2	Read p. 24-27 in reader. *HOMEWORK: Reread p. 24-27 in reader with online **audio**. Complete exercises on p. 46 of workbook.	☐ ☐	(**NEEDED:** Workbook, Teacher's Guide.) **REPEAT Lesson 10 Boardwork Suggestions** on p. 81 as needed. **REVIEW** new vocabulary on p. 43-44 in workbook. **DO Exercises H, I, J** on p. 46 in workbook on the board. *HOMEWORK: Reread p. 24-27 in reader with online **audio**. Complete exercises on p. 46 of workbook.
DAY 3	Read p. 37 in drillbook. *HOMEWORK: Reread the stories on p. 24-27 in **reader** with **audio**. Review B. Grammar Questions on p. 44 of workbook and new vocabulary on p. 43-44 of workbook. Study p. 40 of drillbook.	☐ ☐	(**NEEDED:** Drillbook.) **REVIEW** *"Definitions"* and *"New Vocabulary"* on p. 37 of drillbook. **HAVE** class write **Ego Sum** phrase, both parts of the **Ave Maria** and Lesson 10 saying on the board on p. 40 of the drillbook. *HOMEWORK: Re-read stories on p. 24-27 in **reader** with **audio**. Review B. Grammar Questions on p. 44 of workbook and new vocabulary on p. 43-44 of workbook. Study p. 40 of drillbook.
DAY 4	Lesson 10 Quiz on p. 60 of the **Teacher Guide.**	☐	**LESSON TEN QUIZ:** **VOCABULARY: habitant, stant, ambulant, labōrant, alta, glōriōsa, āra, columna, fenestra, statua** **SUBJECT-VERB AGREEMENT:** Choose 5 sentences from p. 38 of drillbook with cardinal numbers. **LATIN SAYING:** **"Christus ōrat prō nōbīs ut sacerdos."** p. 40, drillbook.

WEEK TWENTY-TWO Grade Book				
ASSIGNMENTS	Include [X]	(A) Points Earned	(B) Possible Points)	A/B x 100 = % (C)
Lesson Ten Quiz	☐		19	
Assignments	☐		6	
WEEK 22 AVERAGE	**Add up column C and divide by number of included [X] assignments =**			

COURSE PLAN (THIRD QUARTER)
WEEK TWENTY-THREE

LATIN
Grade 3

Weekly Breakdown	Goals and Notes for the Week
Predicate nominatives and predicate adjectives, new adjectives, nouns and preposition **prope**.	Understand that predicate nominatives and adjectives are nouns and adjectives that follow a being verb and rename the subject. Must agree with the subject they modify. Learn new vocabulary.

	Student Daily Assignments	[X]	Parent Daily Guidelines
DAY 1	**LESSON ELEVEN** Read p. 47-48 in workbook. *HOMEWORK: Complete p. 47-48 in workbook.	☐ ☐	(**NEEDED:** Workbook.) **READ** *"Predicate Nominatives"* and *"Predicate Adjectives"* on p. 47 of workbook. **WRITE** sentences on the board. **WRITE** new adjectives, nouns and preposition prope on board. **DO** sample sentences from **Exercises A, B, C, D** on p. 48 on the board. *HOMEWORK: Complete p. 47-48 of workbook.
DAY 2	Read p. 28-29 in reader. Read p. 44 in drillbook. *HOMEWORK: Reread p. 28-29 of reader with online **audio**. Complete exercises on p. 44 of drillbook.	☐ ☐	(**NEEDED:** Drillbook, reader, workbook, Teacher's Guide.) **READ** *"New Words To Learn"* on p. 28 of reader and story on p. 29 of reader with class. **INTRODUCE** new **Ego Sum** phrase, the **Gloria Patri** and new Lesson 11 Latin saying on p. 44 of drillbook. *HOMEWORK: Reread p. 28-29 of reader with online **audio**. Complete exercises on p. 44 of drillbook.
DAY 3	Read p. 41-42 in drillbook. *HOMEWORK: Complete the exercises on p. 41-42 in drillbook.	☐ ☐	(**NEEDED:** Drillbook.) **DISCUSS** *"Definitions"* and *"New Vocabulary"* on p. 41 of drillbook. **WRITE** the English cognates from *"Latin-English Cognates"* on p. 41 on the board. **HELP** students find related English words. **READ** *"Origin of Pæninsula"* and *"Mons Ætna"* on p. 42 of drillbook. **HELP** class with *"New Prepositional Phrases"* on p. 42. *HOMEWORK: Complete p. 41-42 in drillbook.
DAY 4	Read p. 49 in workbook. *HOMEWORK: Complete the exercises on p. 49 in workbook.	☐ ☐	(**NEEDED:** Teacher's Guide, workbook.) **DO Lesson 11 Boardwork Suggestions** in Teacher's Guide on p. 80. **DO Exercises E, F, and G** on p. 49 in the workbook on the board with the class. *HOMEWORK: Complete p. 49 in workbook.

WEEK TWENTY-THREE Grade Book

ASSIGNMENTS	Include [X]	(A) Points Earned	(B) Possible Points	A/B x 100 = % (C)
Assignments	☐		8	
WEEK 23 AVERAGE		Add up column C and divide by number of included [X] assignments =		%

Weekly Breakdown		Goals and Notes for the Week
Predicate nominatives and predicate adjectives, new adjectives, nouns and preposition **prope**.		Understand that predicate nominatives and adjectives are nouns and adjectives that follow a being verb and rename the subject. Must agree with the subject they modify. Learn new vocabulary.

	Student Daily Assignments	X	Parent Daily Guidelines
DAY 1	**LESSON ELEVEN** Read p. 43 in drillbook. *HOMEWORK: Complete exercises on p. 43 in drillbook. Study phrase, prayer and saying on p. 44	☐ ☐	(NEEDED: Drillbook.) READ *"Identifying Sentence Elements"* on p. 43 of drillbook. WRITE sentences on the board from *"Sentence Elements Practice"* and have sentences identify sentence elements. *HOMEWORK: Complete p. 43 of drillbook. Study phrase, prayer and saying on p. 44 of drillbook.
DAY 2	Read p. 47, 48, and 50 in the workbook. *HOMEWORK: Complete exercises on p. 50 of workbook.	☐ ☐	(NEEDED: Workbook) REVIEW new adjective, nouns and preposition prope on p. 47-48 in the workbook. DO Exercises H and I on p. 50 on the board with class. *HOMEWORK: Complete exercises on p. 50 of workbook.
DAY 3	Read p. 24-29 in reader. Read p. 37 and 41 in drillbook. *HOMEWORK: Read p. 24-29 in the reader. Review p. 37 and 41 in the drillbook. Study Latin sayings on p. 44 and 48 of drillbook.	☐ ☐	(NEEDED: Drillbook, reader.) RE-READ p. 24-29 in the reader. REVIEW *"Definitions"* and *"New Vocabulary"* on p. 37 and 41 of drillbook. HAVE students write phrases, prayers and saying on p. 40 and 44 in drillbook on the board. *HOMEWORK: Read p. 24-29 in the reader. Review p. 37 and 41 in the drillbook. Study Latin sayings on p. 44 and 48 of drillbook.
DAY 4	Lesson 11 Quiz of p. 61 of the **Teacher Guide**.	☐	**LESSON ELEVEN QUIZ:** VOCABULARY: insula, pæninsula, Ītalia, Mons Ætna, Sicilia, nōta IDENTIFYING Predicate Nominatives and Adjectives: 6 sentences from p. 48 of **workbook** and 4 prepositional phrases with **prope**. LATIN SAYING: "Fēmina tīmēns Dominum laudābitur." p. 44, of the drillbook.

WEEK TWENTY-FOUR Grade Book				
ASSIGNMENTS	Include X	(A) Points Earned	(B) Possible Points	A/B x 100 = % (C)
Lesson Eleven Quiz	☐		17	
Assignments	☐		6	
WEEK 24 AVERAGE		**Add up column C and divide by number of included X assignments =**		%

COURSE PLAN (THIRD QUARTER)
WEEK TWENTY-FIVE

LATIN
Grade 3

Weekly Breakdown	Goals and Notes for the Week
Adjective phrases, adjectives of quantity, declining first declension nouns, new vocabulary.	Learn to recognize adjective phrases. Understand that adjectives of quantity precede the nouns they modify. Begin learning the endings of first declension nouns. Learn new vocabulary.

	Student Daily Assignments [X]	Parent Daily Guidelines
DAY 1	**LESSON TWELVE** Read p. 51-52 in workbook. ☐ *HOMEWORK: Complete p. 51-52 of workbook ☐	(NEEDED: Workbook.) READ *"Adjective Phrases"* on p. 51 in workbook. **WRITE** sentences with adjective phrases on the board. **INTRODUCE** the *"Adjective of Quantity"* **multæ** on p. 51 and new feminine first declension noun **terra**. **DO A. Adjective Phrase Practice** on p. 51 on the board. *HOMEWORK: Complete p. 51-52 of workbook.
DAY 2	Read p. 30-31 in reader. Read p. 48 in drillbook. ☐ *HOMEWORK: Complete the exercises on p. 48 of drillbook.	(NEEDED: Drillbook, reader.) READ *"New Words To Learn"* on p. 30 on reader and story on p. 31. **INTRODUCE** new **Ego Sum** phrase, next phrase of the **Gloria Patrī** and Lesson 12 Latin saying on p. 48 of the drillbook. *HOMEWORK: Complete p. 48 of drillbook. ☐
DAY 3	Read p. 45 and 47 in drillbook. ☐ *HOMEWORK: Complete the exercises on p. 47 of the drillbook. Study phrase, prayer and Lesson 12 Latin saying on p. 48 of drillbook. ☐	(NEEDED: Drillbook.) READ *"Definitions"* and *"New Vocabulary"* on p. 45 of drillbook. **WRITE** the English cognates from *"Latin-English Cognates"* on p. 45 on the board and have students find related Latin words. **READ** *"Terra Incognita"* on p. 45. **DO** *"Sentence Elements Practice"* on p. 47 of drillbook on the board. *HOMEWORK: Complete p. 47 of the drillbook. Study phrase, prayer and Lesson 12 Latin saying on p. 48 of drillbook.
DAY 4	Read p. 52-53 in workbook. ☐ *HOMEWORK: Complete the exercises on p. 53 of the workbook. ☐	(NEEDED: Teacher's Guide, workbook.) **DO LESSON 12 Boardwork Suggestions** on p. 82 of Teacher's Guide. **REVIEW B. Grammar Questions** on p. 52 of workbook. **DO Exercises D, E and F** on p. 53 of the workbook on the board. *HOMEWORK: Complete p. 53 of the workbook.

WEEK TWENTY-FIVE Grade Book				
ASSIGNMENTS	Include [X]	(A) Points Earned	(B) Possible Points)	A/B x 100 = % (C)
Assignments	☐		8	

WEEK 25 AVERAGE	Add up column C and divide by number of included [X] assignments =	%

31

Weekly Breakdown	Goals and Notes for the Week
Adjective phrases, adjectives of quantity, declining first declension nouns, new vocabulary.	Learn to recognize adjective phrases. Understand that adjectives of quantity precede the nouns they modify. Begin learning the endings of first declension nouns. Learn new vocabulary.

	Student Daily Assignments	[X]	Parent Daily Guidelines
DAY 1	**LESSON TWELVE** Read p. 46 of drillbook. *HOMEWORK: Complete the exercises on p. 46 of drillbook. Study phrases, prayers and sayings on p. 40, 44, and 48 of drillbook.	☐ ☐	(NEEDED: Workbook.) **READ** _"Declining First Declension Nouns"_ on p. 46 in drillbook. **MAKE** empty declension charts on p. 46 on the board. **HAVE** students decline first declension feminine nouns with singular endings first, then plural endings. *HOMEWORK: Complete p. 46 of drillbook. Study phrases, prayers and sayings on p. 40, 44, and 48 of drillbook.
DAY 2	Read p. 39-54 in workbook. *HOMEWORK: Complete p. 54 of workbook. Study new vocabulary on p. 51 and Grammer Questions on p. 52 of workbook.	☐ ☐	(NEEDED: Workbook.) **REVIEW** vocabulary on p. 39, 43-44, 47-48 in workbook. **REVIEW B. Grammar Questions** on p. 52 of workbook. **WRITE** sample sentences from **Exercises G, H, and I** on p. 54 on the board and work through them in class. *HOMEWORK: Complete p. 54 of workbook. Study new vocabulary on p. 51 and Grammer Questions on p. 52 of workbook.
DAY 3	Read p. 33- 48 in drillbook. *HOMEWORK: Re-read p. 30-31 in the reader. Review vocabulary and Lesson 12 Latin saying on p. 48 of drillbook	☐ ☐	(NEEDED: Drillbook, reader.) **REVIEW** _"Definitions"_ and _"New Vocabulary"_ on p. 33, 37, 41, and 45 of drillbook. **HAVE** students write on the board the Latin phrases, prayers and sayings on p. 36, 40, 44 and 48 in the drillbook. *HOMEWORK: Re-read p. 30-31 in the reader. Review vocabulary and Lesson 12 Latin saying on p. 48 of drillbook.
DAY 4	Take Lesson 12 Quiz on p. 62 of the Teacher's Guide.	☐	**LESSON TWELVE QUIZ:** **VOCABULARY: terra, multæ** **IDENTIFYING Adjectives of quality:** 5 sentences with **multae**. **FIRST DECLENSION ENDING CHART:** Decline one first declension noun in all 5 cases, singular and plural. **LATIN SAYING:** "Psallat Ecclēsia." p. 48, **drillbook**.

WEEK TWENTY-SIX Grade Book				
ASSIGNMENTS	Include [X]	(A) Points Earned	(B) Possible Points)	A/B x 100 = % (
Lesson Twelve Quiz	☐		15	
Assignments	☐		6	
WEEK 26 AVERAGE	**Add up column C and divide by number of included** [X] **assignments =**			%

WEEK TWENTY-SEVEN

Weekly Breakdown	Goals and Notes for the Week
Comprehensive review of grammar concepts and vocabulary presented in Weeks 19-26.	Review grammar concepts, vocabulary (nouns, adjectives, being verbs, adverbs, conjunctions, prepositions) and practical application for third quarter exam.

Student Daily Assignments [X]	Parent Daily Guidelines
DAY 1 Review Lessons 9-12 in the drillbook. *HOMEWORK: Review "Definitions" and vocabulary from p. 33, 37, 41 and 45 of drillbook. Review the phrases, prayers and sayings from p. 36, 40, 44, and 48 in drillbook. ☐ ☐	(NEEDED: Drillbook, Teacher's Guide) REVIEW sample exercises from the **Boardwork Suggestions** for Lessons 9-12. REVIEW *"Definitions"* and vocabulary from p. 33, 37, 41 and 45 of the drillbook. REVIEW the phrases, prayers and sayings from p. 36, 40, 44 and 48 in drillbook. *HOMEWORK: Review "Definitions" and vocabulary from p. 33, 37, 41 and 45 of drillbook. Review the phrases, prayers and sayings from p. 36, 40, 44, and 48 in drillbook.
DAY 2 Read p. 55-57 workbook. *HOMEWORK: Complete all exercises on p. 55-57 in workbook. ☐ ☐	(NEEDED: Workbook) DISCUSS A. Grammar Review on p. 55 in workbook. DISCUSS sample exercises from p. 56-57 of workbook on the board. *HOMEWORK: Complete all exercises on p. 55-57 in workbook.
DAY 3 Read p. 22-31 in reader. Read p. 58-60 in workbook ☐ *HOMEWORK: Complete p. 58-60 in workbook. Review p. 55-60 in workbook. Study all Latin sayings in drillbook from p. 36, 40, 44, and 48. ☐	(NEEDED: Workbook, reader.) REVIEW p. 22-31 in reader. DISCUSS sample exercises from p. 58-60 in workbook on board with class. HAVE class take turns writing Latin sayings from p. 20, 24, 28, and 32 on the board. *HOMEWORK: Complete p. 58-60 in workbook. Review p. 55-60 in workbook. Study all Latin sayings in drillbook from p. 36, 40, 44, and 48.
DAY 4 Third Quarter Exam on p. 63 of the **Teacher Guide.** ☐	**THIRD QUARTER EXAM**

WEEK TWENTY-SEVEN Grade Book				
ASSIGNMENTS	Include [X]	(A) Points Earned	(B) Possible Points)	A/B x 100 = % (C)
Third Quarter Exam	☐		112	
Assignments	☐		6	
WEEK 27 AVERAGE	Add up column C and divide by number of included [X] assignments =			%

COURSE PLAN (THIRD QUARTER)

	Weekly Averages	Weekly Percent Grade (A)	
Record from Week 19 grades →	Week 19 Average		
Record from Week 20 grades →	Week 20 Average		
Record from Week 21 grades →	Week 21 Average		
Record from Week 22 grades →	Week 22 Average		
Record from Week 23 grades →	Week 23 Average		
Record from Week 24 grades →	Week 24 Average		
Record from Week 25 grades →	Week 25 Average		
Record from Week 26 grades →	Week 26 Average		
Record from Week 27 grades →	Week 27 Average		
Sum of Weekly Percent Grades from Column A =		(B)	
Total Weekly Grade Average	Divide B/8 =	%	
QUARTER 3 LATIN GRADE	Letter Grade Equivalent (see report card) =		

Weekly Breakdown		Goals and Notes for the Week
Prepositional phrases using the ablative and acccusative singular and plural endings.		Learn difference between prepositions **in** and **super**. **In** uses ablative endings; **super** uses accusative endings. Recognize singular and plural ablative and accusative endings. New vocabulary.
Student Daily Assignments	☒	**Parent Daily Guidelines**
DAY 1 — **LESSON THIRTEEN** Read p. 61 in workbook. *HOMEWORK: Complete p. 62 of workbook. Learn **super** and new use of **in**.	☐ ☐	(**NEEDED:** Workbook.) **READ** *"The Preposition In"* on p. 61 of workbook. **WRITE** phrases on board and have class translate them. **INTRODUCE** the preposition **super** on p. 61 and write phrases on board. **TAKE** sample sentences from **Exercises B and C** on p. 62 on the board and work through them with class. *HOMEWORK: Complete p. 62 of workbook. Learn **super** and new use of **in**.
DAY 2 — Read p. 32-33 in reader. Read p. 52 in drillbook. *HOMEWORK: Reread story on p. 32-33 of reader with **audio**. Complete exercises on p. 52 of drillbook.	☐ ☐	(**NEEDED:** Drillbook, reader.) **READ** *"New Words To Learn"* on p. 32 and story on p. 33 of reader. **READ** the new **Ego Sum** phrase, new phrase of the **Gloria Patri** and Lesson 13 Saying on p. 52 of drillbook. *HOMEWORK: Reread story on p. 32-33 of reader with **audio**. Complete exercises on p. 52 of drillbook.
DAY 3 — Read p. 49 in drillbook. *HOMEWORK: Reread stories on p. 32-33 in **reader**. Review **columba**. Complete p. 49-50 in drillbook.	☐ ☐	(**NEEDED:** Drillbook.) **DISCUSS** *"Definitions"* and *"New Vocabulary"* on p. 49 of drillbook. **READ** about new noun **columba** on p. 49. **DO** *"New Prepositional Phrases"* on p. 49 on board with class. **TAKE** sample sentences from exercises on p. 50 in drillbook on the board and work through them with class. *HOMEWORK: Reread stories on p. 32-33 in **reader**. Review **columba**. Complete p. 49-50 in drillbook.
DAY 4 — Read p. 63 in drillbook. *HOMEWORK: Complete exercises on p. 63 in workbook.	☐ ☐	(**NEEDED:** Teacher's Guide, workbook.) **DO LESSON 13 Boardwork Suggestions** on p. 82 of Teacher's Guide. **DO Exercises D and E** on p. 63 of the workbook on the board. *HOMEWORK: Complete p. 63 of the workbook.

WEEK TWENTY-EIGHT Grade Book

ASSIGNMENTS	Include ☒	(A) Points Earned	(B) Possible Points)	A/B x 100 = % (C)
Assignments	☐		8	

WEEK 28 AVERAGE	Add up column C and divide by number of included ☒ assignments =	%

COURSE PLAN (FOURTH QUARTER)
WEEK TWENTY-NINE

LATIN
Grade 3

Weekly Breakdown	Goals and Notes for the Week
Prepositional phrases using the ablative and accusative singular and plural endings.	Learn difference between prepositions **in** and **super**. **In** uses ablative endings; **super** uses accusative endings. Recognize singular and plural ablative and accusative endings. New vocabulary.

	Student Daily Assignments	[X]	Parent Daily Guidelines
DAY 1	**LESSON THIRTEEN** Read p. 50-51 in drillbook. *HOMEWORK: Complete the exercises on p. 50-51 of the drillbook. Study p. 52 of the drillbook.	☐ ☐	(NEEDED: Drillbook.) DO *"Sentence Elements Practice"* on p. 50 of drillbook on the board with class. DRAW a declension chart like the one in *"Declining First Declension Nouns"* on p. 51 of the drillbook on the board. HAVE students write the phrase, prayer and saying on p. 52 of the drillbook on the board. *HOMEWORK: Complete the exercises on p. 50-51 of the drillbook. Study p. 52 of the drillbook.
DAY 2	Read p. 62-64 in workbook. *HOMEWORK: Complete p. 64 of the workbook.	☐ ☐	(NEEDED: Workbook.) READ A. Grammar Questions on p. 62 of workbook with class. REVIEW B. Adjective Phrases on p. 62 and E. Prepositional Phrases on p. 63 of workbook. TAKE sample sentences from Exercises F and G on p. 64 and work through them with class. *HOMEWORK: Complete p. 64 of the workbook.
DAY 3	Read p. 62-63 in the workbook. *HOMEWORK: Reread the stories on p. 32-33 in reader. Review **columba**. Review p. 50- 52 of the drillbook.	☐ ☐	(NEEDED: Teacher's Guide, workbook.) REPEAT Lesson 13 Boardwork Suggestions on p. 82 of Teacher's Guide as needed. REVIEW **super, in** and **columba**. REVIEW A. Grammar Questions on p. 62 of workbook and E. Prepositional Phrases on p. 63 of workbook. *HOMEWORK: Reread stories on p. 32-33 in reader. Review **columba**. Review p. 50- 52 of the drillbook.
DAY 4	Lesson 13 Quiz on p. 69 of the Teacher Guide.	☐	**LESSON THIRTEEN QUIZ:** **VOCABULARY: columba** **PREPOSITIONAL PHRASES**: 6 sentences with **super** and **in**. **GRAMMAR QUESTIONS:** 7 sentences on p. 62 of workbook. **FIRST DECLENSION ENDING CHART:** Decline one first declension noun in all 5 cases, singular and plural (p. 51 of drillbook). **LATIN SAYING:** "Veni, columba mea."

WEEK TWENTY-NINE Grade Book				
ASSIGNMENTS	Include [X]	(A) Points Earned	(B) Possible Points)	A/B x 100 = % (C)
Lesson Thirteen Quiz	☐		20	
Assignments	☐		6	
WEEK 29 AVERAGE	Add up column C and divide by number of included [X] assignments =			%

COURSE PLAN (FOURTH QUARTER)
WEEK THIRTY

Weekly Breakdown	Goals and Notes for the Week
Learn how adjectives must agree with the nouns they modify.	Learn about first and second declension adjectives and what endings are used to modify first declension feminine nouns. New vocabulary.

Student Daily Assignments	X	Parent Daily Guidelines
DAY 1 **LESSON FOURTEEN** Read p. 65-66 in workbook. *HOMEWORK: Complete p. 65-66 in the workbook. Study new vocabulary.	☐ ☐	(**NEEDED:** Workbook.) **READ** *"Adjective/Noun Ageeement"* on p. 65 of workbook. **WRITE** adjective phrase on board and Latin dictionary entry of **albus, -a, -um. INTRODUCE** new vocabulary on p. 65-66. **GO THROUGH** exercises on p. 66 on the board as time permits. *HOMEWORK: Complete p. 65-66 in the workbook. Study new vocabulary.
DAY 2 Read p. 34-37 in reader. Read p. 56 in drillbook. *HOMEWORK: Re-read p. 34-37 in the reader with online audio. Complete p. 56 of the drillbook.	☐ ☐	(**NEEDED:** Drillbook, reader.) **READ** *"New Words To Learn"* on p. 34 and read p. 35-37 in reader. **INTRODUCE** new **Ego Sum phrase**, last phrase of the **Gloria Patri** and Lesson 14 Saying on p. 56 of drillbook. *HOMEWORK: Re-read p. 34-37 in the reader with online audio. Complete p. 56 of the drillbook.
DAY 3 Read p. 53-54 in drillbook. *HOMEWORK: Complete p. 53-54 in the drillbook.	☐ ☐	(**NEEDED:** Drillbook.) **RE-READ** *"Definitions"* and *"New Vocabulary"* on p. 53 of the drillbook. **WRITE** the English cognates from p. 54 on the board and help students find the related Latin cognates from vocabulary list. **READ** about **rubrics** on p. 54. **READ** *"Declining Adjective Phrases"* on p. 54. **MAKE** chart on board. **HELP** students decline **rōsa rubra** (red rose). *HOMEWORK: Complete p. 53-54 in the drillbook.
DAY 4 Read p. 65-67 in workbook. *HOMEWORK: Complete p. 67 in the workbook.	☐ ☐	(**NEEDED:** Teacher's Guide, workbook.) **DO Lesson 14 Boardwork Suggestions** on p. 83 on board with class. **REVIEW** new vocabulary on p. 65 of workbook and **C. Grammar Questions** on p. 66. **DO** sample sentences from **Exercises D and E** on p. 67 of workbook on the board. *HOMEWORK: Complete p. 67 in the workbook.

WEEK THIRTY Grade Book

ASSIGNMENTS	Include X	(A) Points Earned	(B) Possible Points	A/B x 100 = % (C)
Assignments	☐		8	
WEEK 30 AVERAGE	Add up column C and divide by number of included X assignments =			%

COURSE PLAN (FOURTH QUARTER)
WEEK THIRTY-ONE

Weekly Breakdown	Goals and Notes for the Week
Learn how adjectives must agree with the nouns they modify.	Learn about first and second declension adjectives and what endings are used to modify first declension feminine nouns. New vocabulary.

Student Daily Assignments [X]	Parent Daily Guidelines
DAY 1 — **LESSON FOURTEEN** Read p. 53-55 in drillbook. *HOMEWORK: Reread p. 34-37 in the reader with online **audio**. Complete exercises on p. 55 of drillbook. Study p. 56 of the drillbook.	(**NEEDED:** Drillbook.) □ **RE-READ** *"Definitions"* and *"New Vocbulary"* on p. 53 and *"Declining Adjective Phrases"* on p. 54 of the drillbook. **MAKE** declension chart on board and decline **rōsa rubra** and **rōsa alba**. **WRITE** the phrases on p. 55 on the board and help students match pictures with phrases. □ *HOMEWORK: Reread p. 34-37 in the reader with online **audio**. Complete exercises on p. 55 of drillbook. Study p. 56 of the drillbook.
DAY 2 — Read p. 65-68 of workbook. HOMEWORK: Complete p. 68 in the workbook. Study new vocabulary on p. 65-66 and C. Grammar Questions on p. 66 of workbook.	(**NEEDED:** Workbook.) □ **REVIEW** the adjective phrases on p. 66 of the workbook. **WRITE** sample sentences on the board from **Exercises F and G** on p. 68 of the workbook and do them with class. □ *HOMEWORK: Complete p. 68 in the workbook. Study new vocabulary on p. 65-66 and C. Grammar Questions on p. 66 of workbook.
DAY 3 — Read p. 53-56 in drillbook. *HOMEWORK: Re-read p. 34-37 of the reader. Review vocabulary on p. 53 of the drillbook and Latin sayings on p. 56 of the drillbook.	□ (**NEEDED:** Drillbook.) **REPEAT** Lesson 14 Boardwork Suggestions as needed. **REVIEW** the definitions and vocabulary on p. 53 of the drillbook. **HAVE** students write phrases, prayers and saying from p. 52 and 56 of the drillbook on the board. □ *HOMEWORK: Re-read p. 34-37 of the reader. Review vocabulary on p. 53 of the drillbook and Latin sayings on p. 56 of the drillbook.
DAY 4 — Lesson 14 Quiz on p. 70 of the **Teacher Guide**.	**LESSON FOURTEEN QUIZ:** □ **VOCABULARY: alba, densa, rubra, speciōsa, rōsa, murmurat.** **ADJECTIVE PHRASES:** 8 adjective phrases on p. 62 of workbook. **LATIN CARDINAL NUMBERS:** 10 phrases on p. 55 of drillbook. **LATIN SAYING:** "Quasi rosa fructificate." p. 56, drillbook.

WEEK THIRTY-ONE Grade Book

ASSIGNMENTS	Include [X]	(A) Points Earned	(B) Possible Points)	A/B x 100 = % (C
Lesson Fourteen Quiz	□		21	
Assignments	□		6	
WEEK 31 AVERAGE	**Add up column C and divide by number of included [X] assignments =**			%

COURSE PLAN (FOURTH QUARTER)
WEEK THIRTY-TWO

Weekly Breakdown	Goals and Notes for the Week
Learn 6 first declension masculine nouns. Review being verbs and first conjugation endings.	Learn the most common first declension masculine nouns: **agricola, nauta, ıncola, prōphēta, poēta** and **patriarcha** and two new intransitive verbs. Review being verbs in present tense and first conjugation endings.

	Student Daily Assignments	[X]	Parent Daily Guidelines
DAY 1	**LESSON FIFTEEN** Read p. 69-70 in workbook. *HOMEWORK: Complete p. 69-70 in workbook. **workbook** and learn new nouns **agricola, nauta, incola, prōphēta, poēta, patriarcha.**	☐ ☐	(NEEDED: Workbook.) **READ** *"Nouns"* on p. 69 in workbook. **INTRODUCE** 4 new first declension masculine nouns: **agricola, nauta, incola, prōphēta, poēta, patriarcha. INTRODUCE** new verbs on p. 69. **WRITE** sample sentences from **Exercises A and B** on p. 70 on the board and work through them with class. *HOMEWORK: Complete p. 69-70 in workbook and learn new nouns **agricola, nauta, incola, prōphēta, poēta, patriarcha.**
DAY 2	Read p. 38-39 in reader. Read p. 60 in drillbook. *HOMEWORK: Reread story on p. 38-39 of reader with **audio.** Complete exercises on p. 60 of the drillbook.	☐ ☐	(NEEDED: Drillbook and reader.) **READ** *"New Words To Learn"* on p. 38 and story on p. 39 of reader aloud with class. **INTRODUCE** the new **Ego Sum** phrase, the first part of the **Gloria Patri** and the new Week 15 Latin saying on p. 60 of drillbook. *HOMEWORK: Reread story on p. 38-39 of reader with **audio.** Complete exercises on p. 60 of the drillbook.
DAY 3	Read p. 57 in the drillbook. *HOMEWORK: Reread the stories p. 32-39 in the reader with online audio.. Review definitions and vocabulary on p. 49, 53, and 57 in drillbook.	☐ ☐	(NEEDED: Drillbook.) **READ** the *"Definitions"* and *"New Vocabulary"* on p. 57 of the drillbook. **WRITE** the English cognates on p. 57 on the board and help students find related Latin words in the vocabulary list. **READ** the section on **patriarcha** on p. 57 of drillbook aloud with class. *HOMEWORK: Reread stories p. 32-39 in the reader with online audio.. Review definitions and vocabulary on p. 49, 53, and 57 in drillbook.
DAY 4	Read p. 70-71 in the workbook. *HOMEWORK: Complete p. 71 in the workbook.	☐ ☐	(NEEDED: Teacher's Guide and workbook.) **DO Lesson 15 Boardwork Suggestions** on p. 84 of the Teacher's Guide. **REVIEW Exercise B** on p. 70 of workbook on the board. **WRITE** sample sentences from exercises on p. 71 on the board and help students do them. *HOMEWORK: Complete p. 71 in the workbook.

WEEK THIRTY-TWO Grade Book				
ASSIGNMENTS	Include [X]	(A) Points Earned	(B) Possible Points)	A/B x 100 = % (C)
Assignments	☐		8	

WEEK 32 AVERAGE	**Add up column C and divide by number of included** [X] **assignments =**	%

COURSE PLAN (FOURTH QUARTER)

WEEK THIRTY-THREE

Weekly Breakdown		Goals and Notes for the Week
Learn 6 first declension masculine nouns. Review being verbs and first conjugation endings.		Learn the most common first declension masculine nouns: **agricola, nauta, ɪncola, prōphēta, poēta** and **patriarcha** and two new intransitive verbs. Review being verbs in present tense and first conjugation endings.
Student Daily Assignments	X	**Parent Daily Guidelines**
DAY 1	**LESSON FIFTEEN** Read p. 58 of drillbook. *HOMEWORK: Complete p. 58 of drillbook. Study p. 60 of drillbook.	☐ ☐	(NEEDED: Drillbook.) READ "*Third Person Personal Prōnouns*" on p. 58. WRITE the sentences on p. 58 on the board. WRITE the personal prōnouns on the board and have students identify them (see p. 11 of drillbook). REVIEW Latin being verbs on p. 6, 7, and 19 in drillbook. *HOMEWORK: Complete p. 58 of drillbook. Study p. 60 of drillbook.
DAY 2	Read p. 65, 69 and 72 in the workbook. *HOMEWORK: Complete p. 72 in workbook.	☐ ☐	(NEEDED: Teacher's Guide, workbook.) REPEAT Lesson 15 Boardwork Suggestions on p. 84 in the Teacher's Guide as needed. WRITE sample sentences from "*Missing Prepositional Phrases*" on p. 72 on the board and help students work through them. REVIEW vocabulary on p. 65 and 69 in the workbook. *HOMEWORK: Complete p. 72 in workbook.
DAY 3	Read p. 58-60 in drillbook. *HOMEWORK: Complete p. 59 in drillbook. Review Latin Review vocabulary on p. 57 and Latin saying on p. 60 in the drillbook.	☐ ☐	(NEEDED: Drillbook.) REVIEW the personal prōnouns on p. 58 of the drillbook. READ "*More First Conjugation Verbs*" on p. 59 of the drillbook. MAKE charts on p. 59 on the board and have class conjugate verbs, singular forms first, then plural. HELP students with "*First Conjugations Verb Practice*" on p. 59 of the drillbook. HAVE students write Latin phrase, prayer and saying on p. 60 on the board. *HOMEWORK: Complete p. 59 in drillbook. Review Latin Review vocabulary on p. 57 and Latin saying on p. 60 in the drillbook.
DAY 4	Lesson 15 Quiz on p. 71 of the **Teacher's Guide**.	☐	**LESSON FIFTEEN QUIZ:** VOCABULARY: **agrɪcola, nauta, ɪncola, prōphēta, poēta, patriarcha, arat. indāgat.** FIRST CONJUGATION ENDINGS : on p. 59 of drillbook. PRESENT ACTIVE BEING VERBS : on p. 58 of drillbook. LATIN SAYING: "Orāmus semper prō vōbīs." (p. 60 of drillbook.)

WEEK THIRTY-THREE Grade Book					
ASSIGNMENTS	Include	X	(A) Points Earned	(B) Possible Points)	A/B x 100 = % (C)
Lesson Fifteen Quiz	☐			22	
Assignments	☐			6	
WEEK 33 AVERAGE		**Add up column C and divide by number of included** ☒ **assignments =**			**%**

Weekly Breakdown	Goals and Notes for the Week
Review adjective phrases. Know the difference between adjectives of quality and quantity.	Review of adjective phrases. Note difference between adjectives of quality and quantity. Learn new vocabulary: **aqua, nauta, nāvicula, ōra, poēta, vīta, caerulea, natat, nāvigat.**

	Student Daily Assignments	[X]	Parent Daily Guidelines
DAY 1	**LESSON SIXTEEN** Read p. 73-74 in workbook. *HOMEWORK: Complete the exercises on p. 73-74 in workbook.	☐ ☐	(**NEEDED: Workbook.**) **READ** about adjective phrases and *"Adjectives of Quality"* and *"Adjectives of Quantity"* on p. 73. **WRITE** adjective phrases on the board and have class translate. **INTRODUCE** the new vocabulary on p. 73, having students identify nouns, adjectives and verbs. **WRITE** sample phrases and sentences from **Exercises A and B** on p. 74 on board and work through with class. *HOMEWORK: Complete p. 73-74 in workbook.
DAY 2	Read p. 40-44 in reader. Read p. 64 in drillbook. *HOMEWORK: Complete the exercises on p. 64 of the drillbook.	☐ ☐	(**NEEDED: Drillbook, reader.**) **READ** *"New Words To Learn"* on p. 40 and read p. 41-44 of reader aloud in class. **INTRODUCE** new **Ego Sum** phrase, second part of **Gloria Patri** and Week 16 Latin saying on p. 64 in drillbook. *HOMEWORK: Complete exercises on p. 64 of the drillbook.
DAY 3	Read p. 61-62 in drillbook. *HOMEWORK: Complete all exercises on p. 61-62 of drillbook. Study phrase, the **Gloria Patri** and Week 16 Latin saying on p. 64.	☐ ☐	(**NEEDED: Drillbook.**) **DISCUSS** *"Definitions"* and *"New Vocabulary"* on p. 61 of drillbook. **WRITE** English cognates from *"Latin-English Cognates"* on p. 62 on the board and help students find related Latin cognates. **READ** about **poēta** on p. 62. **WRITE** phrases from *"Adjective Phrase Practice"* on p. 62 on the board and help class find matching phrases. *HOMEWORK: Complete all exercises on p. 61-62 of drillbook. Study phrase, the **Gloria Patri** and Week 16 Latin saying on p. 64.
DAY 4	Read p. 73 and 75 in workbook. *HOMEWORK: Complete all exercises on p. 75 of workbook.	☐ ☐	(**NEEDED: Teacher's Guide, workbook.**) **DO Lesson 16 Boardwork Suggestions** on p. 84 of the Teacher's Guide on the board. **REVIEW** vocabulary on p. 73 in workkbook. **WRITE** sample sentences on the board from **Exercises C, D and E** on p. 75 of workbook and help students do them in class. *HOMEWORK: Complete all exercises on p. 75 of workbook.

WEEK THIRTY-FOUR Grade Book				
ASSIGNMENTS	Include [X]	(A) Points Earned	(B) Possible Points)	A/B x 100 = % (C)
Assignments	☐		8	
WEEK 34 AVERAGE	**Add up column C and divide by number of included [X] assignments =**			%

COURSE PLAN (FOURTH QUARTER)
WEEK THIRTY-FIVE

LATIN
Grade 3

Weekly Breakdown	Goals and Notes for the Week
Review adjective phrases. Know the difference between adjectives of quality and quantity.	Review of adjective phrases. Note difference between adjectives of quality and quantity. Learn new vocabulary: **aqua, nauta, nāvicula, ōra, poēta, vīta, caerulea, natat, nāvigat.**

	Student Daily Assignments	[X]	Parent Daily Guidelines
DAY 1	**LESSON SIXTEEN** Read p. 61-63 in drillbook. *HOMEWORK: Complete p. 64 of the drillbook. Review Latin sayings on p. 52, 56, 60 and 64 of drillbook."	☐ ☐	(NEEDED: Drillbook.) **READ** *"Definitions"* and *"New Vocabulary"* on p. 61 with class. **REVIEW** *"Adjective Phrases"* on p. 62 of drillbook on the board. **WRITE** first paragraph from p. 63 on the board and help class find missing verbs. *HOMEWORK: Complete p. 64 of the drillbook. Review Latin sayings on p. 52, 56, 60 and 64 of drillbook.
DAY 2	Read p. 62, 66, 74 and 76 in the workbook. *HOMEWORK: Complete the exercises on p. 76 in the workbook.	☐ ☐	(NEEDED: Teacher's Guide, workbook) **REPEAT** Week 16 Boardwork Suggestions on p. 84 as needed. **DISCUSS A. Grammar Questions** on p. 62 and **C. Grammar Questions** on p. 66 in workbook. **REVIEW A. Matching** and **B. Prepositional Phrases** on p 74 in the workbook. **HAVE** students write them on board and translate. **WRITE** sample sentences from p. 76 on the board and work through them with class. *HOMEWORK: Complete p. 76 in the workbook.
DAY 3	Read p. 32-44 in the reader. Read p. 49, 52-53, 56,-57, 60-61 and 64 in the drillbook. *HOMEWORK: Study definitions, vocabulary on p. 61 and the Week 16 Latin saying on p. 64 of the drillbook.	☐ ☐	(NEEDED: Drillbook, reader.) **RE-READ** p. 32-44 in reader. **REVIEW** definitions and vocabulary from p. 49, 53, 57 and 61 of drillbook. **HAVE** students write **Ego Sum** phrases, the **Gloria Patri** and Lesson 13-16 Latin sayings from p. 52, 56, 60 and 64 in the drillbook on the board. *HOMEWORK: Study definitions, vocabulary on p. 61 and the Week 16 Latin saying on p. 64 of the drillbook.
DAY 4	Lesson 16 Quiz on p. 72 of the **Teacher's Guide.**	☐	**LESSON SIXTEEN QUIZ:** **VOCABULARY: aqua, nauta, nāvicula, ōra, poēta, vīta, caerulea, natat, nāvigat.** **INTRANSITIVE VERBS:** 6 sentences on p. 76 of drillbook. **LATIN SAYING: "Abram habitat in terrā Chanaan."** p. 64, drillbook.

WEEK THIRTY-FIVE Grade Book

ASSIGNMENTS	Include [X]	(A) Points Earned	(B) Possible Points	A/B x 100 = % (C)
Lesson Sixteen Quiz	☐		22	
Assignments	☐		6	
WEEK 35 AVERAGE	**Add up column C and divide by number of included [X] assignments =**			%

COURSE PLAN (FOURTH QUARTER)

LATIN
Grade 3

WEEK THIRTY-SIX

Weekly Breakdown	Goals and Notes for the Week
Comprehensive review of grammar concepts and vocabulary presented in the first seven weeks.	Review grammar concepts, vocabulary (nouns, adjectives, being verbs, intransitive verbs, adverbs, conjunctions, prepositions) and practical application for second quarterly exam.

Student Daily Assignments [X]	Parent Daily Guidelines
DAY 1 **FOURTH QUARTER REVIEW** Review p. 78-80 of workbook. *HOMEWORK: Complete the exercises on p. 77-78 in the workbook.	(**NEEDED:** Workbook.) **REVIEW** vocabulary lists from p. 61, 65-66, 69 and 73 in the workbook. **REVIEW Grammar Questions** on p. 62 and 66. **DISCUSS** the Grammar Questions on p. 77 and vocabulary on p. 78-80. *HOMEWORK: Complete p. 77-80 in the workbook.
DAY 2 Review p. 81-82 in workbook. *HOMEWORK: Complete all the exercises on p. 81-82 of the workbook.	(**NEEDED:** Workbook.) **DISCUSS** sample phrases and subjects on the board with class from the exercises on p. 81-82 of the workbook. *HOMEWORK: Complete all the exercises on p. 81-82 of the workbook.
DAY 3 Read p. 52, 56, 60 and 64 of drillbook. Read p. 83 of the workbook. *HOMEWORK: Complete all the exercises on p. 83 of the workbook. Study p. 78-83 in the workbook.	(**NEEDED:** Workbook.) **DISCUSS** the exercises on p. 83 of the workbook. **WRITE** sample phrases and sentences on the board and work through them with class. **HAVE** students write **Ego Sum** phrases, the **Ave Maria, Signum Crucis** and **Gloria Patri** and the Lesson 13-16 Latin sayings on the board from p. 52, 56, 60 and 64 of the drillbook. *HOMEWORK: Complete all the exercises on p. 83 of the workbook. Study p. 78-83 in the workbook.
DAY 4 Fourth Quarter Exam on p. 73 of the **Teacher Guide**.	**FOURTH QUARTER EXAM**

WEEK THIRTY-SIX Grade Book

ASSIGNMENTS	Include [X]	(A) Points Earned	(B) Possible Points	A/B x 100 = %
Fourth Quarter Exam	☐		101	
Assignments	☐		6	
WEEK 36 AVERAGE		Add up column C and divide by number of included [X] assignments =		%

43

COURSE PLAN (FOURTH QUARTER)

Record from Week 28 grades →	Week 28 Average		
Record from Week 29 grades →	Week 29 Average		
Record from Week 30 grades →	Week 30 Average		
Record from Week 31 grades →	Week 31 Average		
Record from Week 32 grades →	Week 32 Average		
Record from Week 33 grades →	Week 33 Average		
Record from Week 34 grades →	Week 34 Average		
Record from Week 35 grades →	Week 35 Average		
Record from Week 36 grades →	Week 36 Average		
Sum of Weekly Percent Grades from Column A =		(B)	
Total Weekly Grade Average Divide B/8 =		**%**	
QUARTER 4 LATIN GRADE	Letter Grade Equivalent (see report card) =		

WEEKLY QUIZZES AND QUARTER EXAMS

LESSON ONE QUIZ

NAME _____

GRAMMAR DEFINITIONS (Circle the word that best completes each sentence.)

1. (**Nouns / Adjectives**) are words that name persons, places, things or ideas.

2. Latin **nouns** are placed in groups called (**verbs / declensions**).

3. (**First / Second**) declension nouns are Latin nouns which end in **-a** in the nominative singular case.

VOCABULARY (Give the English word for each.)

1. **puella** _____

2. **fēmina** _____

LESSON ONE LATIN SAYING (Give the English translation.)

"O Rōma fēlīx!"

_____

LESSON TWO QUIZ

NAME _____

GRAMMAR DEFINITIONS (Circle the word that best completes each sentence.)

1. The (**subject / verb**) of the sentence is the person, place, or thing a sentence is about.

2. A **subject** is (**singular /plural**) if it is **one** person, place or thing.

3. A **subject** is (**singular /plural**) if it is **more than one** person, place or thing.

4. **Est** is a (**being / transitive**) verb.

5. **Est** is a (**singular / plural**) being verb.

VOCABULARY (Give the English word for each.)

1. **nōn** _____

2. **ancılla** _____

3. **est** _____

MATCHING (Match the Latin being verb with its English equivalent.)

____1. **sum**   **A. we are**

____2. **es**   **B. you (plural) are**

____3. **est**   **C. I am**

____4. **sumus**   **D. you (singular) are**

____5. **estis**   **E. he, she, it is**

____6. **sunt**   **F. they are**

LESSON TWO LATIN SAYING (Give the English translation.)

"**Ego sum resurrectio et vita.**"

_____

LESSON THREE QUIZ

NAME _____

GRAMMAR DEFINITIONS (Circle the word that best completes each sentence.)

1. (**Adjectives / Nouns**) are words that name persons, places or things.

2. Latin nouns are placed in groups called (**declensions / conjugations**).

3. (**First / Second**) declension nouns are Latin nouns which end in **-a** in the nominative singular case.

VOCABULARY (Give the English word for each.)

1. **bona**   _____

2. **Christiāna**   _____

3. **opulenta**   _____

4. **parva**   _____

5. **pulchra**   _____

6. **Rōmāna**   _____

MATCHING (Match the Latin sentence with its English equivalent.)

_____1. **Fēmina est bona.**   **a. She is pretty.**

_____2. **Puella nōn est opulenta.**   **b. The woman is good.**

_____3. **Ancilla nōn est Rōmāna.**   **c. The maidservant is not Roman.**

_____4. **Est pulchra.**   **d. The girl is not wealthy.**

_____5. **Fēmina nōn est Christiāna.**   **e. The woman is not Christian.**

LESSON THREE LATIN SAYING (Give the English translation.)

"Tota pulchra es, Maria."

_____

LESSON FOUR QUIZ

NAME _____

NOMINATIVE PLURALS (Fill in missing forms of the first declension feminine nouns in the nominative case.)

	SINGULAR	PLURAL
NOMINATIVE	1.	**fēminæ**
NOMINATIVE	**ancilla**	2.
NOMINATIVE	**casa**	3.
NOMINATIVE	4.	**viæ**
NOMINATIVE	**villa**	5.
NOMINATIVE	6.	**silvæ**
NOMINATIVE	7.	**ecclēsiæ**
NOMINATIVE	**puella**	8.

VOCABULARY (Give the English word for each.)

1. **ecclēsia** _____

2. **sīlva** _____

3. **vīa** _____

4. **casa** _____

5. **vīlla** _____

LESSON FOUR SAYING (Give the English translation.)

"Viæ vestræ nōn sunt viæ meæ, dīcit Dominus."

_____

QUARTER ONE EXAM

NAME _____

A. GRAMMAR CONCEPTS (Circle the correct **bolded** word in the parentheses.)

1. (**Singular / Plural**) nouns refer to more than one person, place or thing.

2. (**Singular / Plural**) nouns refer to one person, place or thing

3. An (**adjective / adverb**) is a word which describes a noun or prōnoun.

4. (**Nouns / Prepositions**) are words that name persons, places or things.

5. The first declension nominative **singular** ending is (**-a / -æ**).

6. The first declension nominative **plural** ending is (**-a / -æ**).

7. Latin nouns are placed in groups called (**declensions / conjugations**).

8. Most first declension nouns are (**feminine / masculine.**)

9. The (**subject / verb**) is the person, place or thing the sentence is about.

10. **Nōn** is an (**adverb / adjective**).

11. **Et** is a (**conjunction / preposition**) which joins words together.

B. VOCABULARY (Give a definition for each noun, adjective or verb.)

1. **ancilla**   _____

2. **casa**   _____

3. **ecclēsia**   _____

4. **fēmina**   _____

5. **puella**   _____

6. **silva**   _____

7. **via**   _____

8. **villa**   _____

9. **familia**   _____

10. **bona**   _____

11. **Christiāna**   _____

12. **longa**   _____

13. **opulenta**   _____

14. **parva**   _____

15. **pulchra**   _____

16. **Rōmāna**   _____

17. **est**   _____

C. SUBJECTS/ADJECTIVES (Underline subjects and circle adjectives.)

EXAMPLE: <u>Fēmina</u> est (Christiāna.)

1. Puella est Rōmāna.

2. Lūcia nōn est opulenta.

3. Via est longa.

4. Cāsa est parva.

5. Ecclēsia est Christiāna.

6. Ancilla est bona.

D. LATIN-TO-ENGLISH (Give an English translation for each.)

1. Est pulchra.

_____

2. Puella nōn est Rōmāna.

_____

3. Familia est Christiana.

_____

4. Silva nōn est parva.

_____

E. LATIN SAYINGS (Give the English translation.)

1. "O Rōma fēlīx!"

_____

2. "Ego sum resurrectio et vita."

_____

3. "Tota pulchra es, Maria."

_____

4. "Viæ vestræ nōn sunt viæ meæ, dicit Dominus."

_____

LESSON FIVE QUIZ

NAME _____

SENTENCES WITH BEING VERBS (Translate each sentence)

1. Puellæ nōn sunt Rōmānæ.

_____

2. Lūcia est puella bona.

_____

3. Ancillæ sunt Christiānæ.

_____

4. Claudia et Octāvia sunt puellæ Rōmānæ.

_____

5. Ecclēsiæ sunt parvæ.

_____

VOCABULARY (Give the English word for each.)

1. **nōn**   _____

2. est   _____

3. sunt   _____

4. et   _____

LESSON FIVE LATIN SAYING (Give the English translation.)

"Sunt septem ecclēsiæ in Asiā."

_____

LESSON SIX QUIZ

NAME _____

SENTENCES WITH BEING VERBS (Does the verb agrees with the subject?)

1. Puellæ nōn est Rōmānæ.   YES _____   NO _____

2. Fēminae sunt opulentae.   YES _____   NO _____

3. Lūcia et Octāvia est Rōmānae.   YES _____   NO _____

4. Ecclēsia est parva.   YES _____   NO _____

5. Portia et Octāvia sunt Christiānae.   YES _____   NO _____

VOCABULARY (Give the English word for each.)

1. bona _____

2. parva _____

3. opulenta _____

4. pulchra _____

5. Christiāna _____

6. Rōmāna _____

LESSON SIX LATIN SAYING (Give the English translation.)

"Pulchra es et decora, filia Jerusalem."

_____

LESSON SEVEN QUIZ

NAME _____

PREPOSITIONAL PHRASES (Enclose each prepositional phrase in brackets.)

1. Trēs fēminæ Chrīstiānæ sunt in ecclēsiā.
2. Ūna puella est in silvā.
3. Quattuor puellæ Rōmānæ ambulant in viā.
4. Trēs fēminæ sunt in casā.
5. In villā sunt Claudia et Octāvia.

GRAMMAR REVIEW (Circle the bolded word which best completes each sentence.)

1. (In / Ad) may be translated as *in, on* or *upon.*
2. Sunt is a (singular / plural) being verb.
3. Est is a (singular / plural) being verb.
4. The first declension ending (-æ / -a) is plural.
5. The first declenstion ending (-æ / -a) is singular.
6. Non is an (adverb / adjective).
7. Et is a (conjunction / preposition) which joins words together.
8. In is a (conjunction / preposition) showing relationship between words.
9. In silvā is a (conjunction / prepositional phrase.)
10. Adjectives of quality are usually placed (before / after) nouns they modify.
11. A (proper / common) noun denotes a class of objects.
12. A (proper / common) noun names a specific person, place, thing, or idea, spelled with a beginning capital letter.

LESSON SEVEN LATIN SAYING (Give the English translation.)

"Confitēbor tibi in ecclēsiā magnā."

_____

NAME _____

PREPOSITIONAL PHRASES (Enclose each prepositional phrase in brackets.)

1. Fēmina ad ecclēsiam ambulat.
2. Ūna ancilla ad casam ambulat.
3. Puella ad silvam ambulat.
4. Ancilla ad villam ambulat.

VOCABULARY

1. magna _____

2. parva _____

3. antīqua _____

4. splendida _____

5. ambulat _____

6. cantat _____

7. ōrat _____

LATIN EIGHT SAYING (Give the English translation.)

"Cantāte Dominō canticum novum."

_____

QUARTER TWO EXAM

NAME _____

A. GRAMMAR CONCEPTS (Circle the correct **bolded** word in the parentheses.)

1. (**Singular / Plural**) nouns refer to more than one person, place or thing.

2. (**Singular / Plural**) nouns refer to one person, place or thing

3. An (**adjective / adverb**) is a word which describes a noun or prōnoun.

4. (**Nouns / Prepositions**) are words that name persons, places or things.

5. The first declension nominative **singular** ending is (**-a / -æ**).

6. The first declension nominative **plural** ending is (**-a / -æ**).

7. Latin nouns are placed in groups called (**declensions / conjugations**).

8. Most first declension nouns are (**feminine / masculine**.)

9. The (**subject / preposition**) is the person, place or thing the sentence is about.

10. Nōn is an (**adverb / adjective**).

11. **Et** is a (**conjunction / preposition**) which joins words together.

12. **Adjectives of quality** are usually placed (**before / after**) nouns they modify.

13. Latin adjectives (**must / must not**) agree with the nouns they modify in case, number and gender.

14. **Intransitive verbs** (**do / do not**) require an object to complete their meaning.

B. VOCABULARY (Give a definition for each noun, adjective or verb.)

1. **ancilla** _____
2. **casa** _____
3. **ecclēsia** _____
4. **fēmina** _____
5. **puella** _____
6. **silva** _____
7. **via** _____
8. **villa** _____
9. **antīqua** _____
10. **bona** _____
11. **Christiāna** _____
12. **longa** _____

13. **magna** _____
14. **opulenta** _____
15. **parva** _____
16. **pulchra** _____
17. **Rōmāna** _____
18. **splendida** _____
19. **ambulat** _____
20. **cantat** _____
21. **ōrat** _____
22. **est** _____
23. **sunt** _____

C. PREPOSITIONAL PHRASES (Give an English translation for each..)

1. in villā   _____
2. in casā   _____
3. ad ecclēsiam   _____

D. ADJECTIVE PHRASES (Match each phrase with its Latin translation.)

_____1. ancilla bona   A. the Roman women

_____2. ecclēsiæ splendidæ   B. the pretty girl

_____3. puella pulchra   C. a wealthy woman

_____4. fēminæ Rōmānæ   D. a good maidservant

_____5. silva magna   E. small cottages

_____6. casæ parvæ   F. an ancient church

_____7. fēmina opulenta   G. the opulent villas

_____8. viæ longæ   H. a large forest

_____9. villæ opulentæ   I. splendid churches

_____10. ecclēsia antīqua   J. long roads

E. SUBJECTS/ADJECTIVES (Underline subjects and circle adjectives.)

EXAMPLE: <u>Fēmina</u> est (Christiāna).

1. Ecclēsiæ sunt antīquæ.

2. Lūcia est opulenta.

3. Viæ sunt longæ.

4. Silva est magna.

5. Villa est splendida.

6. Casa est parva.

F. LATIN-TO-ENGLISH (Give an English translation for each.) +2 each

1. Est bona.   _____

2. Puellae sunt Rōmānæ.   _____

3. Portia in viā ambulat.   _____

4. In ecclēsia fēmina ōrat.   _____

5. Ancilla cantat.   _____

G. LATIN SAYINGS (Translate each.)

1. "Sunt septem ecclēsiæ in Asiā."

_____

2. "Pulchra es et decora, filia Jerusalem."

_____

3. "Confitēbor tibi in ecclēsiā magnā."

_____

4. "Cantate Dominō canticum novum."

_____

LESSON NINE QUIZ

NAME _____

A. SUBJECT/VERB AGREEMENT (Choose the subject that agrees with the verb.)

1. _____ ambulat.   a. Puellæ   b. Puella
2. _____ cantat.   a. Fēmina   b. Fēminæ
3. _____ volat.   a. Aquila   b. Aquilæ
4. _____ saltat.   a. Puellæ   b. Puella
5. _____ ōrat.   a. Lūcia et Portia   b. Lūcia

B. VOCABULARY (Give an English translation of each.)

1. aquila   _____
2. familia   _____
3. saltat   _____
4. volat   _____
5. stat   _____
6. nova   _____
7. recta   _____

C. LESSON NINE LATIN SAYING (Translate.)

"Quī ambulat simpliciter, ambulat confīdenter."

_____

LESSON TEN QUIZ

NAME _____

SUBJECT/VERB AGREEMENT (Which verb agrees with the subject?)

1. Una puella _____ in ecclēsiā.   a. ōrat   b. ōrant
2. Septem puellæ _____ Rōmānæ.   a. est   b. sunt
3. Trēs ancillæ _____ in villā.   a. labōrat   b. labōrant
4. Familia ad ecclēsiam _____.   a. ambulat   b. ambulant
5. Via _____ antīqua.   a. est   b. sunt
6. Duae aquilae _____.   a. volat   b. volant
7. In casā fēmina _____.   a. habitat   b. habitant
8. Octo columnæ _____.   a. stat   b. stant

VOCABULARY (Give an English translation of each.)

1. āra _____

2. columna _____

3. fenestra _____

4. statua _____

5. alta _____

6. glōriōsa _____

7. habitant _____

8. stant _____

9. ambulant _____

10. labōrant _____

LESSON TEN LATIN SAYING (Translate.)

"Christus ōrat prō nōbīs ut sacerdos."

NAME _____

PREDICATE NOMINATIVES OR ADJECTIVES? (Is the underlined word a
predicate nominative (noun) or a **predicate adjective** (adjective)?

1. Ītalia est <u>pæninsula</u>.   _____
2. Lūcia et Maria sunt <u>puellæ</u>.   _____
3. Mons Ætna est <u>nōta</u>.   _____
4. Fenēstræ sunt <u>glōriōsæ</u>.   _____
5. Ara est <u>splendida</u>.   _____
6. Sicilia est <u>insula</u>.   _____
7. Columnæ sunt <u>altæ</u>.   _____

PREPOSITIONAL PHRASES (Match the correct translations.)

_____1. prope insulam   **A. near the forest**
_____2. prope Ītaliam   **B. near the island**
_____3. prope silvam   **C. near Italy**

VOCABULARY (Give an English translation of each.)

1. pæninsula   _____
2. insula   _____
3. Ītalia   _____
4. Mons Ætna   _____
5. Sicilia   _____
6. nōta   _____

LESSON ELEVEN LATIN SAYING (Translate.)

"Fēmina timēns Dominum laudābitur."

_____

NAME _____

ADJECTIVE PHRASES (Underline each **adjective phrase** and translate.)

EXAMPLE: Multæ columnæ sunt in ecclēsiā.

1. **Est fēmina opulenta.**
2. **Ītalia est pæninsula longa.**
3. **Sicilia est insula nōta.**
4. **Sunt puellæ Rōmānæ.**
5. **Lūcia est puella bona.**

VOCABULARY (Give an English translation of each.)

1. **terra** _____

2. **multæ** _____

DECLINING FIRST DECLENSION NOUNS (Decline the first declension feminine noun **puella** in the chart on the right. The stem is **puēll-**.)

	SINGULAR	PLURAL		SINGULAR	PLURAL
NOMINATIVE	terra	terræ		puella	puellæ
GENITIVE	terræ	terrārum		1.	5.
DATIVE	terræ	terrīs		2.	6.
ACCUSATIVE	terram	terrās		3.	7.
ABLATIVE	terrā	terrīs		4.	puellīs

LESSON TWELVE LATIN SAYING (Translate.)

"Psallat Ecclēsia."

_____

QUARTER THREE EXAM

NAME _____

PART I: GRAMMAR CONCEPTS AND VOCABULARY
A. GRAMMAR QUESTIONS (Circle the correct **bolded** word in the parentheses.)

1. (**Singular / Plural**) nouns refer to more than one person, place or thing.

2. (**Singular / Plural**) nouns refer to one person, place or thing.

3. An (**adjective / adverb**) is a word which describes a noun or prōnoun.

4. (**Nouns / Prepositions**) are words that name persons, places or things.

5. Latin nouns are placed in groups called (**declensions / conjugations**).

6. Most first declension nouns are (**feminine / masculine**.)

7. The (**subject / preposition**) is the person, place or thing the sentence is about.

8. Nōn is an (adverb / adjective).

9. Et is a (conjunction / preposition) which joins words together.

10. An **intransitive verb (does / does not)** require an object to complete its meaning.

11. Present tense means the action is happening (now / in the future.)

12. **Predicate** (nominatives / adjectives) are nouns or prōnouns which follow a being verb and rename or describe the subject.

13. **Predicate** (nominatives /adjectives) are adjectives which follow a being verb and rename or describe the subject.

14. **Third person (singular / plural)** verbs end in **-nt.**

15. "**Third person**" means the (**subject / verb**) is being spoken about.

B. FIRST DECLENSION NOUNS (Define and circle the correct gender.)

1. **ancilla** _____ feminine masculine
2. **aquila** _____ feminine masculine
3. **āra** _____ feminine masculine
4. **casa** _____ feminine masculine
5. **columna** _____ feminine masculine
6. **ecclēsia** _____ feminine masculine
7. **familia** _____ feminine masculine
8. **fēmina** _____ feminine masculine
9. **fenestra** _____ feminine masculine
10. **insula** _____ feminine masculine
11. **Ītalia** _____ feminine masculine
12. **Mons Ætna** _____ feminine masculine
13. **pæninsula** _____ feminine masculine
14. **puella** _____ feminine masculine
15. **Sicilia** _____ feminine masculine
16. **silva** _____ feminine masculine
17. **statua** _____ feminine masculine
18. **terra** _____ feminine masculine
19. **via** _____ feminine masculine
20. **villa** _____ feminine masculine

C. FIRST DECLENSION ADJECTIVES (Give a definition for each adjective.)

1. **alta** _____
2. **antīqua** _____
3. **bona** _____
4. **Christiāna** _____
5. **glōriōsa** _____
6. **longa** _____
7. **magna** _____
8. **multæ** _____
9. **nova** _____
10. **opulenta** _____
11. **parva** _____
12. **pulchra** _____
13. **recta** _____
14. **Rōmāna** _____
15. **splendida** _____

D. INTRANSITIVE VERBS (Define and give the number of each.)

	DEFINITION	*NUMBER*	
1. **ambulat**	_____	singular	plural
2. **ambulant**	_____	singular	plural
3. **cantat**	_____	singular	plural
4. **cantant**	_____	singular	plural
5. **habitat**	_____	singular	plural
6. **habitant**	_____	singular	plural
7. **labōrat**	_____	singular	plural
8. **labōrant**	_____	singular	plural
9. **ōrat**	_____	singular	plural
10. **ōrant**	_____	singular	plural
11. **saltat**	_____	singular	plural
12. **saltant**	_____	singular	plural
13. **stat**	_____	singular	plural
14. **stant**	_____	singular	plural
15. **volat**	_____	singular	plural
16. **volant**	_____	singular	plural

E. BEING VERBS (Define and give the number of each.)

1. **est** _____ singular plural
2. **sunt** _____ singular plural

F. PREPOSITIONS (Define.)

1. **in** _____
2. **ad** _____
3. **prope** _____

G. CONJUNCTION (Define.)

1. **et** _____

H. ADVERB (Define.)

1. **nōn** _____

PART II. PRACTICAL APPLICATION

I. FORMING NOMINATIVE PLURALS (Give the nominative plural form of each first declension feminine noun.)

1. ecclēsia   _____
2. fenestra   _____
3. pæninsula   _____
4. āra   _____
5. insula   _____

J. SUBJECTS AND VERBS (Do the subject and verb agree?)

1. <u>Aquila</u> volant.   Yes _____ No _____
2. Puella ambulat.   Yes _____ No _____
3. <u>Maria et Lūcia</u> labōrant.   Yes _____ No _____
4. <u>Viæ</u> non est rectæ.   Yes _____ No _____
5. <u>Portia</u> saltat.   Yes _____ No _____

K. SUBJECT/VERB AGREEMENT (Circle the verb which agrees with the subject.)

1. Mons Ætna (est / sunt) nōta.
2. Statua (est / sunt) pulchra.
3. In villā familia (habitat / habitant).
4. In silvā aquilæ (volat / volant).
5. Ecclēsia (est / sunt) splendida.

L. PREDICATE NOMINATIVES/ADJECTIVES (Is the underlined word a predicate nominative or a predicate adjective?)

1. Ītalia est <u>paeninsula</u>.   _____
2. Aquila est <u>magna</u>.   _____
3. Vīllæ sunt <u>opulentæ</u>.   _____
4. Portia est <u>ancilla</u>.   _____
5. Mons Ætna est <u>nōta</u>.   _____

M. INTRANSITIVE VERBS (Underline the **verb**. Is it **singular** or **plural**?)

1. Terra est antīqua.   singular   plural
2. In silvā aquilæ volant.   singular   plural
3. Lūcia cantat.   singular   plural
4. Columna stat.   singular   plural
5. Familiæ in ecclēsiā orant.   singular   plural

N. SUBJECT IDENTIFICATION (Draw a line under the <u>subject</u> of each sentence and write it on the line.)

1. Puella in viā ambulat.   _____
2. Ancillæ nōn sunt Rōmānæ. _____
3. Aquilæ volant.   _____
4. Ītalia est pæninsula.   _____
5. Maria et Lūcia cantant.   _____

O. SENTENCE TRANSLATION (Translate each sentence.)

1. Viæ in Sicīliā nōn sunt longæ.

_____

2. Ītalia est terra antīqua.

_____

3. Silvæ sunt magnæ.

_____

4. Familia in pæninsulā habitat.

_____

5. Cantant et saltant.

_____

P. LATIN SAYINGS (Translate each.)

1. "Quī ambulat simpliciter, ambulat confīdenter."

_____

2. "Christus ōrat prō nōbīs ut sacerdos."

_____

3. "Fēmina timēns Dominum laudābitur."

_____

4. "Psallat Ecclēsia."

_____

LESSON THIRTEEN QUIZ

LATIN
Grade 3

NAME _____

GRAMMAR REVIEW (Circle the correct bolded word to complete each sentence.)
1. Adjectives of **quantity** usually go (**before** / **after**) the nouns they describe.
2. Adjectives of **quality** usually go (**before** / **after**) the nouns they describe.
3. Third person (**singular** / **plural**) verbs in **present** tense end in **-t**.
4. Third person (**singular** / **plural**) verbs in **present** tense end in **-nt**.
5. "Third person" means the (**subject** / **verb**) is being spoken about.
6. Predicate (**nominatives** / **adjectives**) are **nouns** or **prōnouns** which follow a being verb and rename or describe the **subject**.
7. Predicate (**nominatives** / **adjectives**) are **adjectives** which follow a being verb and rename or describe the **subject**.

PREPOSITIONAL PHRASES (Match the English phrase with its Latin equivalent.)
___ 1. **over the forests**   **A. super terrās**
___ 2. **over the lands**   **B. super terram**
___ 3. **over the land**   **C. super silvam**
___ 4. **over the forest**   **D. super silvās**

VOCABULARY (Give an English translation.

1. **columba**   _____

DECLINING FIRST DECLENSION NOUNS (Decline the first declension feminine noun **columba** in the chart on the right. The stem is **colūmb-**.)

NOMINATIVE	silva	silvæ		1.	columbæ
GENITIVE	silvæ	silvārum		2.	5.
DATIVE	silvæ	silvīs		3.	columbīs
ACCUSATIVE	silvam	silvās		columbam	6.
ABLATIVE	silvā	silvīs		4.	7.

LESSON THIRTEEN LATIN SAYING (Translate.)
"Venī, columba mea."

NAME _____

ADJECTIVE PHRASES (Match each phrase.)

_____1. the splendid altar   A. columba speciōsa

_____2. a white cottage   B. silva densa

_____3. a red rose   C. alta columna

_____4. the long island   D. fenestra glōriōsa

_____5. a handsome dove   E. āra splendida

_____6. tall column   F. casa alba

_____7. the dense forest   G. rosa rubra

_____8. a glorious window   H. insula longa

VOCABULARY (Give an English translation of these nouns, adjectives and verbs.

1. rosa _____

2. speciosa _____

3. rubra _____

4. alba _____

5. densa _____

6. murmurat _____

LATIN CARDINAL NUMBERS (Match the Latin number phrases with the groups of objects.)

1. _____ 2. _____ 3. _____

4. _____ 5. _____ 6. _____

duae columbæ   octo rosæ   trēs casæ   quattuor fēminæ   quinque puellae   ūna ancilla

LESSON FOURTEEN LATIN SAYING (Translate.)

"Quasi rosa fructificāte."

LESSON FIFTEEN QUIZ

NAME _____

PRESENT ACTIVE BEING VERB (Match the English to the Latin verbs.)

____1. Sumus agricolæ.   A. I am a patriarch.
____2. Estis incolæ.   B. You are a maidservant.
____3. Es ancilla.   C. I am Lucia.
____4. Sum patriarcha.   D. We are farmers.
____5. Sum Lūcia.   E. You all are Roman girls.
____6. Es Octāvia.   F. We are Christian women.
____7. Estis puellæ Rōmānæ.   G. You are Octavia.
____8. Sumus fēminæ Christiānæ.   H. You all are inhabitants.

FIRST CONJUGATION PRESENT ACTIVE (Match English to the Latin verbs.)

labōrō (I work)	labōrāmus 3._____
labōrās 1._____	labōrātis 4._____
labōrat 2._____	labōrant 5._____

you all work
he, she, it works
they work
you work
we work

VOCABULARY (Give an English translation of each.)

1. agricola _____
2. nauta _____
3. incola _____
4. prōphēta _____
5. poēta _____
6. patriarcha _____
7. indāgant _____
8. arant _____

LESSON FIFTEEN LATIN SAYING (Translate.)

"Orāmus semper prō vōbīs."

71

LESSON SIXTEEN QUIZ

NAME _____

SUBJECT/VERB AGREEMENT (Is the underlined verb singular or plural?)

1. Incola in silvā <u>indāgat</u>.   singular   plural
2. Super terram aquilæ <u>volant</u>.   singular   plural
3. Patriarcha in ecclēsiā <u>ōrat</u>.   singular   plural
4. alta columna <u>stat</u>.   singular   plural
5. Poētae in villā splendidā <u>cantant</u>.   singular   plural
6. In aquā cæruleā <u>natant</u>.   singular   plural

LATIN-TO-ENGLISH (Translate the sentences above on lines below.)

1. _____
2. _____
3. _____
4. _____
5. _____
6. _____

VOCABULARY (Give an English translation of each.)

1. **aqua**   _____
2. **nauta**   _____
3. **nāvicula**   _____
4. **ōra**   _____
5. **poēta**   _____
6. **vita**   _____
7. **cærulea**   _____
8. **natat**   _____
9. **nāvigat**   _____

LESSON SIXTEEN LATIN SAYING (Translate.)
   "Abram habitat in terrā Chanaan."

QUARTER FOUR EXAM

NAME _____

PART I: GRAMMAR CONCEPTS AND VOCABULARY
A. GRAMMAR QUESTIONS (Circle the correct **bolded** word in the parentheses.)

1. (**Singular / Plural**) nouns are more than one person, place or thing.

2. (**Singular / Plural**) nouns are one person, place or thing.

3. An (**adjective / adverb**) is a word which describes a noun or prōnoun.

4. (**Nouns / Prepositions**) are words that name persons, places or things.

5. Latin nouns are placed in groups called (**declensions / conjugations**).

6. Most first declension nouns are (**feminine / masculine**.)

7. The (**subject / preposition**) is the person, place or thing the sentence is about.

8. Nōn is an (adverb / adjective).

9. Et is a (conjunction / preposition) which joins words together.

10. An **intransitive verb (does / does not)** require an object to complete its meaning.

11. Present tense means the action is happening (now / in the future.)

12. **Predicate** (nominatives / adjectives) are nouns or prōnouns which follow a being verb and rename or describe the subject.

13. **Predicate** (nominatives /adjectives) are adjectives which follow a being verb and rename or describe the subject.

14. Adjectives of **quantity** usually go (**before / after**) the nouns they describe.

15. Adjectives of **quality** usually go (**before / after**) the nouns they describe.

16. **Third person (singular / plural)** verbs in **present** tense end in **-t.**

17. **Third person (singular / plural)** verbs in **present** tense end in **-nt.**

18. "Third person" means the (**subject / verb**) is being spoken about

19. **First declension masculine nouns** end in (-a / -æ) in the nominative singular.

20. **First declension masculine nouns** end in (-a / -æ) in the nominative plural.

B. FIRST DECLENSION NOUNS (Define and circle correct gender for each nouns.)

1. **aqua** _____ feminine masculine
2. **aquila** _____ feminine masculine
3. **āra** _____ feminine masculine
4. **terra** _____ feminine masculine
5. **columba** _____ feminine masculine
6. **fenestra** _____ feminine masculine
7. **ōra** _____ feminine masculine
8. **nāvicula** _____ feminine masculine
9. **rosa** _____ feminine masculine
10. **vita** _____ feminine masculine
11. **agricola** _____ feminine masculine
12. **nauta** _____ feminine masculine
13. **incola** _____ feminine masculine
14. **patriarcha** _____ feminine masculine
15. **poēta** _____ feminine masculine

C. FIRST AND SECOND DECLENSION ADJECTIVES (Define.)

1. **albus, -a, -um** _____
2. **altus, -a, -um** _____
3. **antīquus, -a, -um** _____
4. **cæruleus, -a, -um** _____
5. **densus, -a, -um** _____
6. **magnus, -a, -um** _____
7. **multus, -a, -um** _____
8. **novus, -a, -um** _____
9. **opulentus, -a, -um** _____
10. **rectus, -a, -um** _____
11. **rubrus, -a, -um** _____
12. **speciōsus, -a, -um** _____

D. INTRANSITVE VERBS (Give a definition for each verb.)

1. arat _____
2. cantat _____
3. arant _____
4. stant _____
5. indāgat _____
6. murmurat _____
7. natant _____
8. nāvigat _____
9. saltant _____
10. habitat _____
11. volant _____
12. volat _____
13. cantant _____
14. habitant _____
15. saltat _____
16. indāgant _____
17. nāvigant _____
18. natat _____
19. murmurant _____
20. stāt _____

E. PREPOSITIONAL PHRASES (Translate each phrase.)

1. prope insulam _____
2. ad ecclēsiam _____
3. in ōrā _____
4. in villā splendidā _____
5. super silvās _____

PART II. PRACTICAL APPLICATION

F. PREDICATE NOMINATIVES / ADJECTIVES (Identify the underlined word as a predicate nominative or predicate adjective.)

1. Aqua est <u>cærulea</u>.   _____

2. Rosa est <u>rubra</u>.   _____

3. Fēminæ sunt <u>opulentæ</u>.   _____

4. Portia est <u>ancilla</u>.   _____

5. Nauta est <u>incola</u>.

G. SUBJECT/VERB AGREEMENT (Do the subjects and verbs agree?)

1. In aqua nautæ navigat.   Yes / No
2. Fenestræ sunt glōriōsæ.   Yes / No
3. In ōrā puella saltat.   Yes / No
4. Super silvās aquilæ volat.   Yes / No
5. Columna sunt alta.   Yes / No

H. LATIN-TO-ENGLISH (Translate each sentence.)

1. Incolæ sunt agricolæ.

_____

2. In ecclēsiā cantant.

_____

3. Viæ nōn sunt longæ.

_____

4. Ītalia est terra antīqua.

_____

5. Rosæ sunt albæ.

_____

I. PREPOSITIONAL PHRASES (Place brackets around <u>prepositional phrases</u>.)

1. Nāviculæ in aquā cæruleā sunt.
2. In Sicīliā nōn sunt viæ rectæ.
3. Prope casam rosæ rubræ sunt.
4. Super silvam aquilæ volant.
5. In terrā agricola arat.

J. FORMING NOMINATIVE PLURALS (Make these nouns plural.)

1. vita   _____
2. columba   _____
3. nauta   _____
4. agricola   _____
5. rosa   _____

K. LATIN SAYINGS (Translate each.)

1. "Venī, columba mea."

_____

2. "Quasi rosa fructificāte."

_____

3. "Orāmus semper prō vōbīs."

_____

4. "Abram habitat in terrā Chanaan."

_____

BOARDWORK SUGGESTIONS *(Puella Romana)*
These may be used as illustrations of the explanations in each lesson.
Read the explanations and examples aloud before the boardwork is attempted.

LESSON ONE: Write this list of first declension nouns on the board. (Prōnunciation given for teacher's use only.) Explain that first declension nouns in the nominative singular end in **-a**. Children may take turns circling the **a** at the end of each noun. These may all be copied into the Latin notebook with other first declension feminine nouns. (The macron, the diacritical mark over the long vowels indicates that the vowel sound should be lengthened or drawn out slightly).

stella (**stel**/lah) star
terra (**tair**/rah) land
insula (**een**/soo/lah) island
glōria (**gloh**/ree/ah) glory
casa (**cah**/sah) cottage, hut
spēlunca (speh/**loon**/cah) cave
tuba (**too**/bah) trumpet

filia (**fee**/lee/ah) daughter
fenestra (feh/**nehs**/strah) window
hora (**oh**/rah) hour
columba (coh/**loom**/bah) dove
statua (**stah**/too/wah) statue
familia (fah/**mee**/lee/ah) family

LESSON TWO: Complete **A. English Practice** on p. 5 of workbook on the board, helping the students identify the subject of each sentence. Give examples of sentences with common and proper nouns: *Susan is reading a book. Europe is a continent. Mount Rushmore is a monument in South Dakota. Abraham Lincoln was the 16th president.*

LESSON THREE: Write these English sentences on the board and have the students take turns underlining the subjects and circling the (predicate) adjectives: *The sky is cloudy. The soldier is brave. The saints were virtuous. Jeremiah was hungry. China is large. The radio is loud. George Washington was polite. Susan is industrious. The cat is watchful. The ship is enormous.* Now write these Latin sentences and have the students identify subjects and adjective in same manner. If there is any difficulty, remind students that the subject is doing the action. (Subjects may also have action done to them with passive verbs.) The (predicate) adjectives give information about the subject. Remember that **nōn** is an adverb.
1. Octāvia est pulchra. (Octavia is Roman.)
2. Ancilla est Christiāna. (The maidservant is Christian.)
3. Lūcia nōn est opulenta. (Lucia is not wealthy.)
4. Fēmina est bona. (The woman is good.)
5. Puella est Rōmāna. (Puella is Roman.)

If more sentences are needed, the subjects and adjectives are interchangeable.

LESSON FOUR: Complete **A. Plural Practice** on p. 14 of workbook on the board. Make a chart with two columns, "SINGULAR" and "PLURAL". Write each Latin noun in the nominative singular on the board and have students take turns forming the nominative plural of each. Explain that the **root stem** of the noun is the part of the word without the ending:

fēmin + -a = fēmina	**ecclēsi + -a = ecclēsia**	**vi + -a = via**
fēmin + -æ = fēminæ	**ecclēsi + -æ = ecclēsiæ**	**vi + -æ = viæ**
puell + -a = puella	**famili + -a = familia**	**silv + -a = silva**
puell + -æ = puellæ	**famili + -æ = famīliæ**	**silv + -æ = silvæ**
ancill + -a = ancilla	**cas + -a = casa**	**vill + -a = villa**
ancill + -æ = ancillæ	**cas + -æ = casæ**	**vill + -æ = villæ**

LESSON FIVE: Write each sentence as shown and have students take turns circling the correct verb in each. More examples:

1. Ancilla (est / sunt) bona. (est) *The maid is good.*
2. Ancillæ (est / sunt bonae. (sunt) *The maids are good.*
3. Lūcia (est / sunt) Christiāna. (est) *Lucia is Christian.*
*4. Lūcia et Octāvia (est / sunt) Christiāna. (sunt) *Lucia and Octavia are Christian.*
5. Puella (est / sunt) parva. (est) *The girl is small.*
6. Puellæ (est / sunt) parvae. (sunt) *The girls are small.*
*7. Claudia et Octāvia (est / sunt) (sunt) puellae. *Claudia and Octavia are girls.*
*8. Ancilla et fēmina nōn (est / sunt) (sunt) Rōmānae. *The maidservant and the woman are not Roman.*
9. Fēmina nōn (est / sunt) opulenta. (est) *The woman is not wealthy.*
10. Fēminæ (est / sunt) Christiānæ. (sunt) *The women are Christians.*

* Explain that Sentences 4, 7, and 8 have compound subjects: two nouns joined by the conjunction

    Lūcia et Octāvia (Lucia and Octavia)
    Claudia et Octāvia (Claudia and Octavia)
    Ancilla et fēmina (the maidservant and the woman)

LESSON SIX: Write each sentence as shown and have students take turns circling the adjective and underlining the noun it modifies. Write these sentences and have students circle the subjects and adjectives:

1. Puella est pulchra. (The girl is beautiful.)
2. Puellæ sunt pulchræ. (The girls are beautiful.)
3. Ancilla nōn est Rōmāna. (The maidservant is not Roman.)
4. Ancillæ nōn sunt Rōmānæ. (The maidservants are not Roman.)
5. Fēmina est opulenta. (The woman is wealthy.)
6. Fēminæ sunt opulentæ. (The women are wealthy.)
7. Antōnia est Christiāna. (Antonia is Christian.)
8. Antōnia et Lūcia sunt Christiānæ. (Antonia and Lucia are Christian.)
9. Via est longa. (The road is long.)
10. Viae sunt longæ. (The roads are long.)

LESSON SEVEN: Copy the prepositional phrases on p. 27 in workbook on the board and have students circle the preposition and identify the object of the preposition in each phrase. (The object of the preposition **in** is governed by the **ablative** case so the object of the preposition must be in the ablative case. This is indicated by the **-ā** with a diacritical symbol, the macron, which means it is in the first declension ablative singular. This means the vowel sound must be lengthened or drawn out slightly. Latin prepositions vary in the case that they are governed by. They are usually governed by the ablative or accusative cases.)

in viā = in (preposition) + viā (object of preposition) (on the road)
in ecclēsiā = in (preposition) + ecclēsiā (object of preposition) (in the church)
in terrā = in (preposition) + terrā (object of preposition) (on the land)
in silvā = in (preposition) + silvā (object of preposition) (in the forest)
in casā = in (preposition) + cāsā (object of preposition) (in the cottage)

Explain to students that the Latin preposition **in** may be translated as *in, on, or upon*, depending on the context of the sentence.

LESSON EIGHT: Copy the prepositional phrases on p. 31 in workbook on the board and have students circle the preposition and identify the object of the preposition in each phrase. (The object of the preposition **ad** is governed by the accusative case so the object of the preposition must be in the accusative case. Accusative singular ending in the first declension is **-am**. Latin prepositions vary in the case that they are governed by. They are usually governed by the ablative or accusative cases.)

ad villam = ad (preposition) + villam (object of preposition) (to the villa)
ad ecclēsiam = ad (preposition) + ecclēsiam (object of preposition) (to the church)
ad silvam = ad (preposition) + silvām (object of preposition) (to the forest)
ad casam = ad (preposition) + casam (object of preposition) (to the cottage)

Explain that, unlike English use, adjectives are usually placed **after** the nouns they modify unless they are adjectives of quantity which we will study later. Write these singular adjective phrases on the board and have the children form the plural forms by replacing the ending -**a** with the dipthong -**æ**.

ecclēsia antīqua (ancient church)	ecclēsiæ antīquæ (ancient churches)
via longa (long road)	viæ longæ (long roads)
silva magna (large forest)	silvæ magnæ (large forests)
villa splendida (splendid villa)	villæ splendidæ (splendid villas)
puella Rōmāna (Roman girl)	puellæ Rōmānæ (Roman girls)
fēmina Christiāna (Christian woman)	fēminæ Christiānæ (Christian women)
ancilla bona (good maidservant)	ancillæ bonæ (good maidservants)

New simple verbs in the lesson are intransitive verbs which do not require an object to complete their meaning. These are in the third person singular so they can only be used with singular subjects (ending in -a). They may stand alone; in that case the subject is translated as "he, she, or it", depending on the context of the sentence. The verb is usually placed at the end of the sentence.

ambulat = he walks, she walks, or it walks
cantat = he sings, she sings, or it sings
ōrat = he prays, she prays, or it prays

When combined with nouns as subjects, the prōnoun he, she or it is dropped. Write these on the board and have the children take turns giving an English translation. Any variety of these subjects and verbs may be used.

Ancilla cantat. (The maid sings.)
Puella ambulat. (The girl walks.)
Fēmina ōrat. (The woman prays.)

Prepositional phrases may also be added:

In viā puella ambulat. (The girl walks on the road.)
In casā ancilla cantat. (The maid sings in the cottage.)
In ecclēsiā fēmina ōrat. (The woman prays in the church.)

LESSONS ONE THROUGH EIGHT REVIEW
The review in the workbook may be used as preparation for the Quarter One examination.

LESSON NINE: Have students take turns going to the board and writing the Latin translation of these simple sentences with the third person singular intransitive verbs: **habitat, ambulat, saltat, stat, volat, cantat, ōrat.** If English-to-Latin is too difficult, try Latin-to-English.

1. He prays. (Ōrat.)
2. She walks. (Ambulat.)
3. Maria sings. (Maria cantat.)
4. The maid walks. (Ancilla ambulat.)
5. The woman prays. (Fēmina ōrat.)
6. She dances. (Saltat.)
7. The church is large. (Ecclēsia est magna.)
8. The woman is good. (Fēmina est bona.)
9. She lives. (Habitat.)
10. The girl stands. (Puella stat.)
11. Lūcia dances. (Lūcia saltat.)
12. It flies. (Volat.)

LESSON TEN: Explain that third person (indicative active) singular verbs end in **-t,** and third person (indicative active) plural verbs end in **-nt.** If these verbs are used on their own, the subject is "they". However, if used with a subject noun, "they" is dropped. Write these plural intransitive verbs on the board:

habitant (they live)   volant (they fly)
stant (they stand)   labōrant (they work)
ambulant (they walk)   saltant (they dance)
cantant (they sing)
ōrant (they pray)

Help the students combine these nouns in the nominative plural (ending in -æ) and compound subjects with the plural verbs above to make new simple sentences:

puellæ (girls)   Lūcia et Octāvia
fēminæ (women)   puella et fēmina
ancillæ (maids)   Claudia et Antonia
aquilæ (eagles   Lūcia et Portīa et Octāvia
famīliæ (families)

Examples: Aquilæ volant. Puellæ saltant. Ancillæ labōrant.

Use the plural being verb **sunt** with the following plural nouns and adjectives to make sentences with being verbs:

NOUNS		ADJECTIVES	
puellæ (girls)	ecclēsiæ (churches)	pulchræ (pretty)	antīquæ (ancient)
fēminæ (women)	āræ (altars)	bonæ (good)	glōriōsæ (glorious)
ancillæ (maids)	fenestræ (windows)	magnæ (large)	splendidæ (splendid)
aquilæ (eagles)	columnæ (columns)	parvæ (small)	Rōmānæ (Roman)
famīliæ (families)	statuæ (statues)	novæ (new)	Christiānæ (Christian)
viæ (roads)		rectæ (straight)	opulentæ (wealthy)
villæ (villas)		altæ (tall)	longæ (long)

Remember that **altæ** is an adjective of quantity so it must stand before the noun. Some examples of sentences with being verbs: Aquilæ sunt magnæ. Viæ sunt rectæ. Statuæ sunt pulchræ.

LESSON ELEVEN: Explain that in sentences with being verbs the subject is usually followed by a **predicate complement** which gives further information about the subject. The **predicate complement** is called a **predicate nominative** if it is a noun, and a **predicate adjective** if it is an adjective.

Write these sentences on the board and ask the students to find identify the underlined word as a predicate adjective or predicate nominative:

> Mons Ætna est <u>nōta</u>. (Mount Etna is <u>famous</u>.) (predicate adjective)
> Insulæ sunt <u>parvæ</u>. (The islands are <u>small</u>.) (predicate adjective)
> Ītalia est <u>pæninsula</u>. (Italy is a <u>peninsula</u>.) (predicate nominative)
> Fēminæ nōn sunt <u>opulentæ</u>. (The women are not <u>wealthy</u>.) (predicate adjective)
> Sicilia est <u>insula</u>. (Sicily is an <u>island</u>.) (predicate nominative)
> Fenestra est <u>glōriōsa</u>. (The window is <u>glorious</u>.) (predicate adjective)
> Portia est <u>ancilla</u>. (Portia is a <u>maid</u>.) (predicate nominative)

Explain that the new preposition, prope (near), like ad, is a preposition whose objects must be in the accusative case: **prope Ītaliam** (near Italy). Have students translate these prepositional phrases: *prope insulam, prope casam, prope silvam, prope ecclēsiam.*

LESSON TWELVE: Have students take turns going to the board and writing the Latin translation of these phrases with the adjective of quantity, **multus, -a, -um,** *many,* which must stand before the nouns it modifies:

1. many islands (multæ insulæ)
2. many girls (multæ puellæ)
3. many women (multæ fēminæ)
4. many peninsulas (multæ pæninsulæ)
5. many lands (multæ terræ)
6. many churches (multæ ecclēsiæ)
7. many villas (multæ villæ)
8. many roads (multæ viæ)
9. many columns (multæ columnæ)
10. many maidservants (multæ ancillæ)
11. many eagles (multæ aquilæ)
12. many windows (multæ fenestræ)
13. many cottages (multæ casæ)

LESSON THIRTEEN: Explain that prepositional phrases that have plural objects will have a different ending. With the preposition **in,** whose object must be in the **ablative** case, the first declension ablative **plural** ending is -īs. Make sure to point out the diacritical mark above the ī which means the vowel sound is lengthened. Some examples to write on the board: *in silvīs, in casīs, in villīs, in insulīs, in paeninsulīs, in ecclēsiīs.*

With the new preposition **super** *(over, above)* whose object must be in the **accusative** case, the first declension accusative **plural** ending is -ās. Make sure to point out the diacritical mark above the ā which means the vowel sound is lengthened. Some examples of prepositional phrases with plural objects using **super**: *super silvās, super terrās, super insulās, super viās, super casās.*

Write the following prepositional phrases on the board to illustrate the difference in singular and plural objects in the ablative and accusative cases and ask students to give translations:

PREPOSITIONAL PHRASES WITH OBJECTS IN ABLATIVE CASE

IN + ABLATIVE
in silvā (in the forest)
in silvīs (in the forests)
in villā (in the villa)
in villīs (in villas)
in casā (in the cottage)
in casīs (in the cottages)
in ecclēsiā (in the church)
in ecclēsiīs (in the churches)

AD + ACCUSATVE
ad ecclēsiam (to the church)
ad ecclēsiās (to the churches)
ad casam (to the cottage)
ad casās (to the cottages)
ad silvam (to the forest)
ad silvās (to the forests)
ad villam (to the villa)
ad villās (to the villas)

PREPOSITIONAL PHRASES WITH OBJECTS IN ACCUSATIVE CASE

SUPER + ACCUSATIVE
super silvam (over the forest)
super silvās (over the forests)
super terram (over the land)
super terrās (over the lands)
super insulam (near the island)
super insulās (near the islands)
super ecclēsiam (near the church)
super ecclēsiās (near the churches)

PROPE + ACCUSATIVE
prope insulam (near the island)
prope insulās (near the islands)
prope casam (near the cottage)
prope casās (near the cottages)
prope ecclēsiam (near the church)
prope ecclsias (near the churches)
prope silvam (near the forest)
prope silvas (near the forests)

Explain that objects of prepositional phrases may sometimes have adjectives that modify them included in the phrase. If the noun object of a preposition requires an adjective, the adjective must agree with the noun in **case, gender** and **number.** With first declension feminine nouns and adjectives, the endings of nouns and adjectives will match exactly, but this will not always be the case! Some examples to write on the board:

PREPOSITIONAL PHRASES WITH ADJECTIVES

in ecclēsiā splendidā (in the splendid church)
in ecclēsiīs splendidīs (in the splendid churches)
in casā parvā (in the small cottage)
in casīs parvīs (in the small cottages)
in silvā densā (in the dense forest)
in sīlvis dēnsīs (in the dense forests)

ad silvam magnam (to the large forest)
ad silvas magnās (to the large forests)
ad ecclēsiam antīquam (to the ancient church)
ad ecclēsias antīquās (to the ancient churches)
super silvam densam (over the dense forest)
super silvam densās (over the dense forests)

83

LESSON FOURTEEN: Review with students the concept that adjectives must agree with the nouns they modify in case, gender and number. This is called adjective/noun agreement. If a noun is feminine, the adjective modifying it must use a feminine ending. If the noun is singular, the adjective modifying it must also have a singular ending. Whatever case the noun is in must be shared by the adjective.

Thus, nominative (case) singular (number) feminine (gender) nouns are modified by nominative singular feminine adjectives. By extension ablative singular feminine nouns must be modified by ablative singular feminine adjectives, and accusative singular feminine nouns must be modified by accusative singular feminine adjectives.

Write the following nominative singular feminine nouns on the board and ask the students to offer appropriate nominative singular feminine modifying adjectives. (Both noun and adjective endings will match in these cases, but nouns/adjective agreement does not always mean the endings will match exactly.)

SINGULAR NOUNS		POSSIBLE ADJECTIVES
ecclēsia _____	(church)	magna, antīqua, splendida, parva, Christiāna
columba _____	(dove)	speciōsa, alba, parva
puella _____	(girl)	pulchra, opulenta, parva, Christiāna, bona, Rōmāna
fēmina _____	(woman)	(same as above)
rosa _____	(rosa)	alba, rubra, speciōsa, splendida
silva _____	(forest)	densa, magna, parva, antīqua, speciōsa
fenestra _____	(window)	magna, parva, splendida, glōriōsa
āra _____	(altar)	magna, parva, nova, splendida, pulchra, antīqua
aquila _____	(eagle)	magna, parva, speciōsa
statua _____	(statua)	pulchra, glōriōsa, splendida, speciōsa, magna
via _____	(road)	longa, antīqua, recta, nova
columna _____	(column)	alta, recta, nova

The same may be done with plural nouns. Multæ (many) can be used with plural nouns.

LESSON FIFTEEN: Introduce the students to the concept of masculine nouns which are nouns that are considered to be male or have male characteristics. There are only a few masculine nouns in the first declension. The majority of masculine nouns are in the second declension and end in **-us** or **-r**. Some first declension masculine nouns are: agricola (farmer), nauta (sailor), incola (inhabitant), patriarcha (patriarch), scrība (writer), poēta (poet) pirāta (pirate), and prōphēta (prophet). Review the new intransitive verbs on p. 69 so the students can translate these sentences on the board.

Write these on the board and ask students to translate. If students can do this easily, reverse the order and have them give English-to-Latin translations:

Agricola arat. (The farmer plows.)
Agricolæ arant. (The farmers plow.)
Incola indāgat. (An inhabitant hunts.)
Incolæ indāgant. (Inhabitants hunt.)
Columba murmurat. (A dove murmurs (coos).)
Columbæ murmurant. (Doves murmur (coo).)
Fēmina saltat. (The girl dances.)
Fēminæ saltant. (The girls dance.)
Columna stat. (The column stands.)
Columnæ stant. (The columns stand.)

Āra stat. (The altar stands.)
Āræ stant. (The altars stand.)
Aquila volat. (The eagle flies.)
Aquilæ volant. (The eagles fly.)
Ancilla labōrat. (The maid works.)
Ancillæ labōrant. (Maids work.)
Patriarcha ōrat and cantat. (The patriarch prays and sings.)
Patriarchæ ōrant et cantant. (Patriarchs pray and sing.)
Puella cantat et saltat. (The girl sings and dances.)
Puellæ cantant et saltant. (The girls sing and dance.)

Ask the students to circle all the new first declension masculine nouns above. (agricola, incola, patriarcha)

LESSON SIXTEEN: Write these adjective phrases on the board and ask students to translate: via recta (straight road), villa nova (new villa), columba speciōsa (beautiful dove), fenestra glōriōsa (glorious window), aquila magna (large eagle), alta columna (tall column), āra alba (white altar), rosa rubra (red rose) aqua caerulea (blue water), vita speciōsa (beautiful life), ōra longa (long beach), nāvicula alba (white boat).

As a final review, write these sentences on the board and give these directions:

1. In terra agricolæ <u>arant</u>. (On the land the farmers <u>plow</u>.) *Underline the intransitive verb.*
2. <u>Nautæ</u> nāvigant in nāviculīs. (Sailors sail in boats.) *Underline the subject.*
3. Multæ rosæ prope casam <u>sunt</u>. (Many roses are near the cottage.) *Underline the being verb.*
4. Incola est <u>agricola</u>. (The inhabitant is a <u>farmer</u>.) *Underline the predicate nominative.*
5. <u>In villa</u> ancilla labōrat. (<u>In the villa</u> the maid works.) *Underline the prepositional phrase.*
6. Columnæ sunt <u>altæ</u>. (The columns are <u>tall</u>.) *Underline the predicate adjective.*
7. In Siciliā viæ <u>nōn</u> sunt rectæ. (The roads are <u>not</u> straight in Sicily.) *Underline the adverb.*
8. Saltant <u>et</u> cantant. (They sing <u>and</u> dance.) *Underline the conjunction.*
9. Sicilia est <u>prope Ītaliam</u>. (Sicily is near Italy.) *Underline the prepositional phrase.*
10. <u>Lūcia et Portia</u> sunt puellæ. (Lūcia and Portia are girls.) *Underline the compound subject.*
11. <u>In aqua cærulea</u>, puellæ natant. (<u>In the blue water</u>, the girls swim). *Underline the prepositional phrase.*
12. Aquila volat. (The eagle flies.) *Underline the subject.*
13. Columbæ <u>albæ</u> murmurat. (The white doves murmur.) *Underline the adjective.*
14. Rosa <u>est</u> rubra. (The rose is red.) *Underline the being verb.*
15. <u>Multæ</u> aquilæ volant super silvās. (<u>Many</u> eagles fly over the forests.) *Underline the adjective.*

ANSWER KEY

LESSON ONE QUIZ, p. 46
GRAMMAR DEFINITIONS
1. Nouns
2. declensions
3. First

VOCABULARY
1. girl
2. woman

LESSON ONE LATIN SAYING
O happy Rome!

LESSON TWO QUIZ, p. 47
GRAMMAR DEFINITIONS
1. subject
2. singular
3. plural
4. being
5. singular

VOCABULARY
1. not
2. maidservant
3. he, she, it is

MATCHING
1. C. I am
2. D. you (sing.) are
3. E. he, she, it is
4. A. we are
5. B. you (plural) are
6. F. they are

LESSON TWO LATIN SAYING
I am the Resurrection and the Life.

LESSON THREE QUIZ, p. 48
GRAMMAR DEFINITIONS
1. Nouns
2. declensions
3. First

VOCABULARY

1. good
2. Christian
3. wealthy, grand
4. small
5. pretty, beautiful
6. Roman

MATCHING

1. B. The woman is good.
2. D. The girl is not wealthy.
3. C. The maidservant is not Roman.
4. A. She is pretty.
5. E. The woman is not Christian.

LESSON THREE LATIN SAYING

Thou art all beautiful, O Mary.

LESSON FOUR QUIZ, p. 49
NOMINATIVE PLURALS

1. fēmina (woman)
2. ancillæ (maidservants)
3. casæ (cottages)
4. via (road, way)
5. villæ (villas)
6. silva (forest)
7. ecclēsia (church)
8. puellæ (girls)

VOCABULARY

1. church
2. forest
3. road, way
4. cottage
5. villa, manor

LESSON FOUR LATIN SAYING

Thy ways are not my ways, says the Lord.

QUARTER ONE EXAM, p. 50
A. GRAMMAR CONCEPTS

1. Plural
2. Singular
3. adjective
4. Nouns
5. -a
6. -æ

7. declensions
8. feminine
9. subject
10. adverb
11. conjunction

B. VOCABULARY
1. maidervant
2. cottage
3. church
4. woman
5. girl
6. forest
7. way, road
8. villa, manor
9. family
10. good
11. Christian
12. long
13. wealthy, grand
14. small
15. pretty, beautiful
16. Roman
17. he, she, it is

C. SUBJECT/ADJECTIVES, p. 51
1. <u>Puella</u> est Rōmāna. (The girl is Roman.)
2. <u>Lūcia</u> nōn est opulenta. (Lucia is not wealthy.)
3. <u>Via</u> est longa. (The road is long.)
4. <u>Cāsa</u> est parva. (The cottage is small.)
5. <u>Ecclēsia</u> est Christiāna. (The church is Christian.)
6. <u>Ancilla</u> est bona. (The maidservant is good.)

D. LATIN-TO-ENGLISH
1. She is pretty.
2. The girl is not Roman.
3. The family is Christian.
4. The forest is not small.

E. LATIN SAYINGS
1. O happy Rome!
2. I am the Resurrection and the Life.
3. Thou art all beautiful, O Mary.
4. Thy ways are not my ways, says the Lord.

LESSON FIVE QUIZ, p. 52
SENTENCES WITH BEING VERBS
1. The girls are not Roman.
2. Lucia is a good girl.
3. The maidservants are Christian.
4. Claudia and Octavia are Roman girls.
5. The churches are small.

VOCABULARY
1. not
2. he, she, it is
3. they are
4. and

LESSON FIVE LATIN SAYING
There are seven churches in Asia.

LESSON SIX QUIZ, p. 53
SENTENCES WITH BEING VERBS
1. No.
2. Yes.
3. No.
4. Yes.
5. Yes.

VOCABULARY
1. good
2. small
3. wealthy
4. pretty, beautiful
5. Christian
6. Roman

LESSON SIX LATIN SAYING
Thou art beautiful and pleasing, O daughter of Jerusalem.

LESSON SEVEN QUIZ, p. 54
PREPOSITIONAL PHRASES
1. [in ecclēsiā] Three Christian women are [in the church].
2. [in silvā] One girl is [in the forest].
3. [in viā] Four Roman girls walk [on the road].
4. [in casā] Three women are [in the cottage].
5. [in villā] Claudia and Octavia are [in the villa].

GRAMMAR REVIEW, p. 54
1. In
2. plural
3. singular

4. -æ
5. -a
6. adverb
7. conjunction
8. preposition
9. prepositional phrase
10. after
11. common
12. proper

LESSON SEVEN LATIN SAYING
I shall give Thee thanks in the great church.

LESSON EIGHT QUIZ, p. 55
PREPOSITIONAL PHRASES
1. [ad ecclēsiam] The woman walks [to the church].
2. [ad casam] One maidservant walks [to the cottage].
3. [ad silvam] The girl walks [to the forest].
4. [ad villam] The maidservant walks [to the villa].

VOCABULARY
1. great, large
2. small
3. ancient, old
4. splendid, shining
5. he, she, it walks
6. he, she, it sings
7. he, she, it prays

LESSON EIGHT LATIN SAYING
Sing to the Lord a new song.

QUARTER TWO EXAM, p. 56
A. GRAMMAR CONCEPTS
1. Plural
2. Singular
3. adjective
4. Nouns
5. -a
6. -æ
7. declensions
8. feminine
9. subject
10. adverb
11. conjunction
12. after

13. must
14. do not

B. VOCABULARY
1. maidservant
2. cottage
3. church
4. woman
5. girl
6. forest
7. road, way
8. villa, manor
9. old, ancient
10. good
11. Christian
12. long
13. great, large
14. wealthy, grand
15. small
16. pretty, beautiful
17. Roman
18. splendid, shining
19. he, she, it walks
20. he, she, it sings
21. he, she, it prays
22. he, she, it is
23. they are

C. PREPOSITIONAL PHRASES, p. 57
1. in the villa
2. in the cottage
3. to the church

D. ADJECTIVE PHRASES
1. D. a good maidservant
2. I. splendid churches
3. B. the pretty girl
4. A. the Roman women
5. H. a large forest
6. E. small cottages
7. C. a wealthy woman
8. J. long roads
9. G. the opulent villas
10. F. an ancient church

E. SUBJECTS/ADJECTIVES
1. Ecclēsiæ sunt antīquæ. (The churches are ancient.)

2. Lūcia est opulenta. (Lucia is wealthy.)

92

3. <u>Viæ</u> sunt longæ. (The roads are long.)

4. <u>Silva</u> est magna. (The forest is large.)

5. <u>Villa</u> est splendida. (The villa is splendid.)

6. <u>Casa</u> est parva. (The cottage is small.)

F. LATIN-TO-ENGLISH

1. She is good.
2. The girls are Roman.
3. Portia walks on the road.
4. A woman prays in the church.
5. The maidservant sings.

G. LATIN SAYINGS, p. 58

1. There are seven churches in Asia.
2. Thou art beautiful and pleasing, O daughter of Jerusalem.
3. I shall give Thee thanks in the great church.
4. Sing to the Lord a new song.

LESSON NINE QUIZ, p. 59
SUBJECT/VERB AGREEMENT

1. b. Puella
2. a. Fēmina
3. a. Aquila
4. b. Puella
5. b. Lūcia

VOCABULARY

1. eagle
2. family
3. he, she, it dances
4. he, she, it flies
5. he, she, it stands
6. new
7. straight

LESSON NINE LATIN SAYING

He that walketh sincerely, walketh confidently.

LESSON TEN QUIZ, p. 60
SUBJECT/VERB AGREEMENT

1. a. ōrat
2. b. sunt
3. b. labōrant
4. a. ambulat
5. a. est
6. b. volant
7. a. habitat
8. b. stant

VOCABULARY
1. altar
2. column
3. window
4. statue
5. tall
6. glorious
7. they live
8. they stand
9. they walk
10. they work

LESSON TEN LATIN SAYING
Christ prays for us as a priest.

LESSON ELEVEN QUIZ, p. 61
PREDICATE NOMINATIVES OR ADJECTIVES?
1. predicate nominative
2. predicate nominative
3. predicate adjective
4. predicate adjective
5. predicate adjective
6. predicate nominative
7. predicate adjective

PREPOSITIONAL PHRASES
1. B. near the island
2. C. near Italy
3. A. near the forest

VOCABULARY
1. peninsula
2. island
3. Italy
4. Mount Etna
5. Sicily
6. famous

LESSON ELEVEN LATIN SAYING
The woman fearing the Lord shall be praised.

LESSON TWELVE QUIZ, p. 62
ADJECTIVE PHRASES
1. fēmina opulenta (wealthy woman)
2. pæninsula longa (long peninsula)
3. insula nōta (famous island)
4. puellæ Rōmānæ (Roman girls)
5. puella bona (good girl)

VOCABULARY

1. land, country
2. many

DECLINING FIRST DECLENSION NOUNS

1. puellæ
2. puellæ
3. puellam
4. puēllā
5. puellārum
6. puellīs
7. puēllās

LESSON TWELVE LATIN SAYING

Let the Church chant the psalms.

QUARTER THREE EXAM, p. 63
PART I. GRAMMAR CONCEPTS AND VOCABULARY
A. GRAMMAR QUESTIONS

1. Plural
2. Singular
3. adjective
4. Nouns
5. declensions
6. feminine
7. subjects
8. adverb
9. conjunction
10. does not
11. now
12. nominatives
13. adjectives
14. plural
15. subject

B. FIRST DECLENSION NOUNS, p. 64

1. maidservant (feminine)
2. eagle (feminine)
3. altar (feminine)
4. cottage (feminine)
5. column (feminine)
6. church (feminine)
7. family (feminine)
8. woman (feminine)
9. window (feminine)
10. island (feminine)
11. Italy (feminine)
12. Mount Etna (feminine)
13. peninsula (feminine)

14. girl (feminine)
15. Sicily (feminine)
16. forest (feminine)
17. statue (feminine)
18. land, country (feminine)
19. road, way (feminine)
20. villa, manor (feminine)

C. FIRST DECLENSION ADJECTIVES
1. tall
2. old, ancient
3. good
4. Christian
5. glorious
6. long
7. large, great
8. many
9. new
10. wealthy, grand
11. small
12. pretty, beautiful
13. straight
14. Roman
15. splendid, shining

D. INTRANSITIVE VERBS, p. 65
1. he, she, it walks (singular)
2. they walk (plural)
3. he, she, it sings (singular)
4. they sing (plural)
5. he, she, it lives (singular)
6. they live (plural)
7. he, she, it works (singular)
8. they work (plural)
9. he, she, it prays (singular)
10. they pray (plural)
11. he, she, it dances (singular)
12. they dance (plural)
13. he, she, it stands (singular)
14. they stand (plural)
15. he, she, it flies (singular)
16. they fly (plural)

E. BEING VERBS
1. he, she, it is (singular)
2. they are (plural)

F. PREPOSITIONS
1. in, on, upon
2. to, toward

3. near

G. CONJUNCTION
1. and

H. ADVERB
1. not

PART II. PRACTICAL APPLICATION, p. 66
I. FORMING NOMINATIVE PLURALS
1. ecclēsiæ
2. fenestræ
3. pæninsulæ
4. āræ
5. insulæ

J. SUBJECTS AND VERBS
1. No.
2. Yes.
3. Yes.
4. Yes.
5. Yes.

K. SUBJECT/VERB AGREEMENT
1. est
2. est
3. habitat
4. volant
5. est

L. PREDICATE NOMINATIVES/ADJECTIVES
1. predicate nominative
2. predicate adjective
3. predicate adjective
4. predicate nominative
5. predicate adjective

M. INTRANSITIVE VERBS, p. 67
1. est (singular)
2. volant (plural)
3. cantat (singular)
4. stat (singular)
5. ōrant (plural)

N. SUBJECT IDENTIFICATION
1. Puella
2. Ancillæ
3. Aquilæ
4. Ītalia

5. Maria et Lūcia

O. SENTENCE TRANSLATION
1. The roads in Sicilia are not long.
2. Italy is an ancient land.
3. The forests are large.
4. The family lives on the peninsula.
5. They sing and dance.

P. LATIN SAYINGS, p. 68
1. He that walketh sincerely, walketh confidently.
2. Christ prays for us as a priest.
3. The woman fearing the Lord shall be praised.
4. Let the Church chant the psalms.

LESSON THIRTEEN QUIZ, p. 69
GRAMMAR REVIEW
1. before
2. after
3. singular
4. plural
5. subject
6. nominatives
7. adjectives

PREPOSITIONAL PHRASES
1. D. super silvās
2. A. super terrās
3. B. super terram
4. C. super silvam

VOCABULARY
1. dove

DECLINING FIRST DECLENSION NOUNS
1. columba
2. columbæ
3. columbæ
4. columbā
5. columbārum
6. columbās
7. columbīs

LESSON THIRTEEN LATIN SAYING
Come away, my dove.

LESSON FOURTEEN QUIZ, p. 70
ADJECTIVE PHRASES
1. E. āra splendida
2. F. casa alba
3. G. rosa rubra
4. H. insula longa
5. A. columba speciōsa
6. C. alta columna
7. B. silva densa
8. D. fenestra glōriōsa

VOCABULARY
1. rose
2. beautiful, handsome
3. red
4. white
5. dense
6. he, she, it murmurs, coos

LATIN CARDINAL NUMBERS
1. ūna ancilla
2. quattuor fēminæ
3. duæ columbæ
4. trēs casæ
5. quinque puellæ
6. octo rosæ

LESSON FOURTEEN LATIN SAYING
Bloom ye like a rose.

LESSON FIFTEEN QUIZ, p. 71
PRESENT ACTIVE BEING VERB
1. D. We are farmers.
2. H. You all are inhabitants.
3. B. You are a maidservant.
4. A. I am a patriarch.
5. C. I am Lucia.
6. G. You are Octavia.
7. E. You all are Roman girls.
8. F. We are Christian women.

FIRST CONJUGATION PRESENT ACTIVE, p. 71
1. labōrās (you work)
2. labōrat (he, she, it works)
3. labōrāmus (we work)
4. lāborātis (you all work)
5. labōrant (they work)

VOCABULARY
1. farmer
2. sailor
3. inhabitant
4. prōphet
5. poet
6. patriarch
7. they hunt
8. they plow

LESSON FIFTEEN LATIN SAYING
We always pray for you.

LESSON SIXTEEN QUIZ, p. 72
SUBJECT/VERB AGREEMENT
1. singular
2. plural
3. singular
4. singular
5. plural
6. plural

LATIN-TO-ENGLISH
1. The inhabitant hunts in the forest.
2. The eagle flies over the land.
3. The patriarch prays in the church.
4. A tall column stands
5. Poets sing in the splendid villa.
6. They swim in the blue water.

VOCABULARY
1. water
2. sailor
3. little boat
4. shore
5. poet
6. life
7. blue
8. he, she, it swims
9. he, she, it sails

LESSON SIXTEEN LATIN SAYING
Abram lives in the land of Canaan.

QUARTER FOUR EXAM, p. 73
PART I: GRAMMAR CONCEPTS AND VOCABULARY
A. GRAMMAR QUESTIONS
1. Plural
2. Singular
3. adjective
4. Nouns
5. declensions
6. feminine
7. subject
8. adverb
9. conjunction
10. does not
11. now
12. nominatives
13. adjectives
14. before
15. after
16. singular
17. plural
18. subject
19. -a
20. -æ

B. FIRST DECLENSION NOUNS, p. 74
1. water (feminine)
2. eagle (feminine)
3. altar (feminine)
4. land, country (feminine)
5. dove (feminine)
6. window (feminine)
7. shore (feminine)
8. little boat (feminine)
9. rose (feminine)
10. life (feminine)
11. farmer (masculine)
12. sailor (masculine)
13. inhabitant (masculine)
14. patriarch (masculine)
15. poet (masculine)

C. FIRST AND SECOND DECLENSION ADJECTIVES
1. white
2. tall
3. old, ancient
4. deep blue
5. dense, thick
6. large, great
7. many

8. new
9. wealthy, grand
10. straight
11. red
12. beautiful, handsome

D. INTRANSITIVE VERBS, p. 75
1. he, she, it plows
2. he, she, it sings
3. they plow
4. they stand
5. he, she, it hunts
6. he, she, it murmurs, coos
7. they swim
8. he, she, it sails
9. they dance
10. he, she, it lives
11. they fly
12. he, she, it flies
13. they sing
14. they live
15. he, she, it dances
16. they hunt
17. they sail
18. he, she, it swims
19. they murmur, coo
20. he, she, it stands

E. PREPOSITIONAL PHRASES
1. near the island
2. to the church
3. on the shore
4. in the splendid villa
5. over the forests

PART II: PRACTICAL APPLICATION, p. 76
F. PREDICATE NOMINATIVES/ADJECTIVES
1. predicate adjective
2. predicate adjective
3. predicate adjective
4. predicate nominative
5. predicate nominative

G. SUBJECT/VERB AGREEEMENT
1. No.
2. Yes.
3. Yes.
4. No.
5. No.

H. LATIN-TO-ENGLISH

1. The inhabitants are farmers.
2. They sing in the church.
3. The roads are not long.
4. Italy is an ancient land.
5. The roses are white.

I. PREPOSITIONAL PHRASES, p. 77

1. [in aquā cæruleā] The boats are [in the blue water].
2. [In Siciliā] There are not straight roads [in Sicily].
3. [prope casam] There are red roses [near the cottage].
4. [super silvam] The eagles fly [over the forest].
5. [in terrā] The farmer plows [on the land].

J. FORMING NOMINATIVE PLURALS

1. vītæ
2. columbæ
3. nautæ
4. agricolæ
5. rosæ

K. LATIN SAYINGS

1. Come away, my dove.
2. Bloom ye like the rose.
3. We always pray for you.
4. Abram lives in the land of Canaan.

Made in the USA
Middletown, DE
22 April 2023

28916903R00060